LIVING
a better
STORY

Living a Better Story
Published by Franklin Green Publishing
P.O. Box 2828
Brentwood, Tennessee 37024

Cover design by Marc Pewitt

Photography: Cover photo provided by Brentwood UMC;
photo on page 131, Marc Pewitt

ISBN 978-1-93648-709-7

Printed in the United States of America

LIVING
a better
STORY

Brentwood United Methodist Church

Carol Bumbalough, Editor

FRANKLIN GREEN
PUBLISHING
Brentwood, Tennessee

CONTENTS

FOREWORD

WHEN WE STARTED this Living A Better Story journey in January of this year, never could we have realized what would come from it. Never could we have anticipated the passion and creativity people would put into seeking to live a better story.

And the stories you told! Stories as wonderful as hosting a lemonade stand in your front yard and as dramatic as the Living A Better Story experience leading to an adoption of a child from Ethiopia. Amazing!

But what you may not be fully aware of is how our story is affecting others. From the seed we planted in launching the Living A Better Story experience, others have been inspired and are doing so as well. Other churches, private Christian schools and Universities around the United States are either committing to or considering having a Living A Better Story experience. Why so much interest in getting a $5, $10, or $20 with the challenge to go make a difference? We believe it's because deep down inside each of us is the desire to live a better story, a desire to be used by God in some way that helps people's lives and makes the world a better place. What God has brought forth from you is an experience that I would call an "inciting incident" that helps people jumpstart a really great story.

We are so proud of what we have done together. We live in a world so cynical about the church and its motives in our world. We live in a world not motivated by religious commitment and institutional dedication, but by compassion, community, and hope. The Living A Better Story experience is a beacon for those who seek to live their Christian faith not by the law, but by love.

In these pages you will find many individual stories, stories that will move you, make you think, make you laugh, make you cry. But just as important as the collection of these stories in this book and the stories lived but not written down, is your story together. This is the story of Brentwood United Methodist Church. This is the story of our church seeking to live out the great God story to make a difference in the world. This is Brentwood United Methodist Church living a better story.

There are more stories to be written, lives to be touched and transformed. Please know your story has made our story better.

—*The Staff of Brentwood United Methodist*

Some trust in chariots and some in horses, but we trust
in the name of the LORD our God.
Psalm 20:7

A WORD OF THANKS

THE RESPONSE to Living a Better Story was overwhelming! We received so many beautiful stories—stories of generosity, of trust, of delightful surprises. Regrettably, we were unable to publish all of them. To everyone who participated in Living a Better Story and who responded to our request to share your experience, we say a heartfelt "Thank you!" We pray that you were blessed as you prayed, listened, and trusted.

I am no longer my own, but thine.

Put me to what thou wilt, rank me with whom thou wilt.

Put me to doing, put me to suffering.

Let me be employed for thee or laid aside for thee,

exalted for thee or brought low for thee.

Let me be full, let me be empty.

Let me have all things, let me have nothing.

I freely and heartily yield all things to thy pleasure and disposal.

And now, O glorious and blessed God, Father, Son and Holy Spirit,

thou art mine, and I am thine.

So be it.

And the covenant which I have made on earth,

let it be ratified in heaven.

Amen.

—JOHN WESLEY

Offering Ourselves

FTER TALKING, PRAYING, AND SEARCHING for the perfect cause for us, we decided on drug addiction and domestic violence. We decided to add to our $15 from our savings. That was a stretch, as Gordy has been unemployed for over a year and things are very tight! Drug addiction and domestic violence are not subjects we knew much about until this past year. Both have affected our family in recent months. For people who had never dealt with such horrors, they were now at our back door. What a helpless feeling.

We talked and talked about the funds going to a drug facility. We did some research but could not find a specific center. One Sunday we were in the car on our way to church, and I decided to call a number I found for a local drug center here in Williamson County. I called the number and was told that they would not be able to help me at that location but that someone would call in a few days and maybe they could direct me. When we got to church that morning, we found that Cliff was taking time to ask the congregation to share their stories. The very last gentleman who spoke was named John, and he said he worked with people who had addictions. Gordy and I looked at each other in shock. He said he was trying to put together funds and start some type of organization to help people with additions to enter a rehab facility when they did not have the money to do so. God sent his answer to us by way of a fellow church member! God returned our call! We spoke to John after church and told him of our situation and that we wanted to give to his story. He explained that he was trying to get things started and felt that he might need to start a 501(c)(3) but had not that done as yet because he was still in the research stage. Because I work for a bank and do that type of work, I told him that I had that information at my fingertips. I offered to help him open the account and do anything I could to get things started.

We felt good about our decision but believed that we would have given so much more had we been in better place financially. But being financially challenged makes you creative, so we came up with another idea. We called Bridges of Williamson County and offered ourselves. We do not have much money, but we can give of ourselves to those in need. We are now on their volunteer list. Gordy will be able to help them with their auto needs whenever necessary, and we are on their on-call list to pick up donated food and clothing.

If it had not been for the $15 that was given to us in those envelopes, we would never have been motivated to do these wonderful deeds.

—*Gordy and Andrea Schnarrs*

Payne Family Blessings

MY THIRTEEN-YEAR-OLD son Robby and I are leaving for Ethiopia, Africa, all because of a $35 gift. Here's why...

A few months back our church handed us an envelope containing $35. They asked us to multiply the gift and then to give it away. The rules were that it had to go outside the walls of our church. I knew immediately that I wanted to help Amazima Ministries, which was begun by a twenty-one-year-old woman from Brentwood (kissesfromkatie.blogspot.com). Our family organized a garage sale (collecting donations from friends and family), and the kids set up a breakfast stand. They sold sausage biscuits and juice, and we raised $563 for Amazima Ministry. I began reading Katie's blog regularly, and it made me desire to minister to children in Africa. All of a sudden, raising money for her ministry did not seem to be enough. I have heard people say that God has laid something on their hearts before, but I have never experienced anything like it until now. I learned about the orphans in Africa, and it touched me deeply.

The thought of a child not being tucked in at night, not having a parent or anyone in the world to care and love them, not having someone to tell them how smart and beautiful they are, not having anyone to show them the love that Jesus has for them just made my heart hurt...and YEARN! This is how our journey started.

I have a loving husband who supports me and loves me to the end of the earth. I have two beautiful children who are becoming passionate about adoption and willing to give LOVE to someone they have never met, someone who does not have a "forever family." I have a son who said he had a dream that he had a dark-skinned brother. This is where our journey starts, and we are hungry for what tomorrow brings! Shout out to my grandma who taught me to "Put it in God's hands!" Well, grandma, I think I will do just that! We will just see what his plans are.

We are praying and believing that God is speaking to us to adopt a child from Ethiopia. My husband and I are always open to adoption (again), but we have never taken any action. Our children, Robby and Caitlin, were adopted shortly after we were married. This $35 gift led us to get involved with a local nonprofit, something we had been meaning to do. The $35 gift allowed us to not put it off any longer. This is where our journey started, and it is still going. So we're off to Ethiopia to see where God's path leads.

"I have heard people say that God laid something on their hearts before, but I have never experienced anything like it until now."

We were raised as Christians, but honestly we have been lukewarm with our involvement. This journey has strengthened our belief, our love, and need for God. We are trusting and relying on him to lead us. We have trusted him to provide a means to do all that we have done thus far, and he has provided it. This has taught us to be more obedient, to be more faithful, and to listen. I am forever grateful for this chance to be part of the Living a Better Story journey! We have grown in our faith, opened the hearts of others, spread word of the orphan crisis in the world, and have taught our kids and ourselves how good it feels to give to others. We are so blessed and thankful for this opportunity. We are so excited to see where God leads us.

—*Gina and Phillip Payne*

Tips for Sight

I RECEIVED A $20 gift in the Living Better Story envelope and invested it in faith after praying for three days. I work part time in a barbershop and decided to use my tips for the first day to begin the earnings for the faith mission.

I later placed a jar on the counter with a note that said "God's Money" and prayed for God to move people to add to the amount. After one week I had received $221. I sent the money to a medical mission in Honduras to cover the cost of having a young girl's eyes treated for several weeks. The money was such a blessing as well as a miracle. I truly learned that even though we may feel overwhelmed with the needs around us, God can multiply our efforts and bring blessings to many people.

Thanks for allowing me to share in this great blessing and to witness God at work.

—*James R. Lamb*

Waiting for a Flood of Blessings

WITH ALL OF THE stories coming out of the 2010 flood, we felt compelled to make a difference in someone's life by volunteering and spiritual and financial gifts. My wife Lisa spent a Saturday helping a family in Ashland City clean out their home. While she and several other people helped to clean up, a FEMA representative came by and notified Andy and Jackie (the homeowners) that their home fell in the flood way and that they would not be allowed to rebuild their home of thirty years. This was tremendously distressing to them because they had just paid off the mortgage on the home. Knowing that they needed the support more than the cleaning, everyone stayed and helped the rest of the afternoon. On the way home Lisa felt the Lord talking to her about this couple, and after a family discussion we decided this was the story we had been waiting to live. Both our boys, Ryan and Michael, chipped in, and our yard sale came quickly to fruition.

We at first felt that we had procrastinated on this project, but we soon realized that God had saved our efforts to help this couple that was so devastated by this event. It has been a blessing to all four of us.

—*Mike Dennison*

Presents and Peaches

WE WERE ORIGINALLY GIVEN $20. Bob multiplied his money by asking our family not to give him a birthday present but rather cash donations for this project. Everyone was so generous when they heard about Living a Better Story. He collected $220 from his birthday presents. Next, I auctioned off a basket of fried peach pies for the cause and collected $60. This, added to the original $20, totaled $300, which was given to the Bethesda Center in Ashland City.

"If we handled all of our money and gifts with such care and thoughtfulness, I am sure that we could live a bigger, better story."

We felt like we were truly doing something special for God. It was very difficult deciding what to do with the money because there are so many needs in our area at this time. We felt like the original $20 was very sacred to us. If we handled all of our money and gifts with such care and thoughtfulness, I am sure that we could live a bigger, better story. This is pretty cool: another family member wants only money for his birthday next month so that he can Live a Better Story too.

—*Bob and Trina Chance*

A Recipe for Living a Better Story

A FEW MONTHS AGO I provided the Women of Hope Center in Pinson, Tennessee, near Jackson, with a very special recipe for cream pie from my great-great aunt Becky Taylor, who was in a family of Methodist ministers. This recipe has been in my family for over a hundred years, and the women there are using it to make pies to raise money for the operation of the center.

After prayerful consideration, I decided to use the $5 I received in the envelope at BUMC to buy some ingredients for making those pies for which I had provided the recipe. Here is how that will multiply: they can make at least three pies with the $5 of ingredients, and the proceeds will be $30, since they sell the pies for $10 each. The next week they will use the seed money and proceeds for ingredients for eighteen pies and the proceeds will be $180, and the process will continue as long as there is demand for the pies.

Women of Hope is a faith-based retreat for women in Jackson and the surrounding areas who are suffering with alcohol and drug addictions. The program offers Christian discipleship, screening and access to services, faith-based support groups, individual mentoring, family support groups, transportation and housing, case management, a continuing support plan, job placement assistance, and continuing education.

—*Lucinda Hall*

A Home and a Family

I STARTED WITH $5 on February 21 and it multiplied to $250. After praying for almost a week, the calling my family and I had was to help the Tennessee Children's Home in Spring Hill. The big need there this year is for four defibrillators for their four locations in the state. They each cost $1,800, a total of $7,200. They hope to raise the money by June 30. Bill, an employee at the organization, said that any amount would help. He and I talked for a long time, and he asked me why I chose the Tennessee Children's Home. I told him my story.

I was adopted when I was ten days old. Although there have been struggles in my life at times, I know that I was truly blessed to be adopted. In high school I often struggled with why I was having to go through some of the things that my family had dealt with over the years (my parents divorced when I was five years old, my brother died when I was nine years old, and then my mom and stepdad divorced while I was in high school).

I had a Bible teacher in high school who knew I was struggling, and one day she pulled me aside after class and told me, "God brought you into this world for a reason. He has a plan for your life, so do not mess it up!" Although I had grown up in the church, I had not really felt God's love until then. At that moment I realized that God did love me and had a plan for my life.

This April I will be thirty-three, and I still think of my birth mother often. I do not know anything about her or anything about the circumstances surrounding my birth or adoption, but I am so thankful that she made the choice to give me up for adoption. I know that it was God's plan. I have very loving adoptive parents, stepparents, and my sister (who was also adopted), and I am now blessed with two children of my own (the first blood relatives I have ever known!).

I admire the Tennessee Children's Home in Spring Hill for providing such a wonderful Christian environment for the orphaned, abused, and neglected children they help. I wanted to do my part to give back to them. I could have just gone over there and given them the $5, but I wanted to do more! The goal is to raise $7,200 for them by the end of June. My company is going to match the money that we raise, and I am planning two community events (a family barbecue supper fund-raiser and a fund-raising night dedicated to the Tennessee Children's Home at a local restaurant, which will donate 10 to 15 percent of their sales for the Tennessee Children's Home in April and May to help raise more money.

This Living a Better Story experience has been great! My kids have asked so many questions about the children who live at the Tennessee Children's Home. I have always been open with my kids about my adoption, and although it has been hard for them to understand sometimes, I know that this experience has truly helped them understand a little more. In their nightly prayers they always thank God especially for mommy, and to me that means the world.

Thank you for this wonderful opportunity. I know in the coming weeks and months that we will continue to reach out to the Tennessee Children's Home to help the children who are not as fortunate as I was to have adoptive parents.

—*Mary McGaughey*

School Supplies

OW, WHAT AN INTERESTING, fun, and challenging assignment we were given! Our family was given $10 and told that it was God's money to be invested into his kingdom. We were told to come up with ways to make the money multiply. Our heads were flooded with ideas!

After prayerful and careful consideration, discussion, and debate, we still found ourselves with too many good ideas of how to use God's money! There is just so much need in the world, and it's easy to feel overwhelmed when you want to be helpful. We had recently watched a documentary about the lost boys, refugees from war-torn Africa who had resettled in America and were sending their earnings to their impoverished home countries. We had read about efforts to improve squalid conditions at an orphanage in China. We had heard heartbreaking stories about the earthquake in Haiti. It seemed as though we were being bombarded with images of need from around the world, and we were starting out with just $10. As we thought about the fact that human needs know no nationalities or borders, we kept coming back to the wonderful work of the United Methodist Committee on Relief (UMCOR).

One of the ways to help UMCOR is by putting together relief supply kits. We used our $10 for supplies that will be part of one of UMCOR's school kits. In some countries, children do not have the most basic school supplies. Many have no schoolrooms; classes are held in inadequate or half-destroyed buildings, tents, or even the open air. School kits may be the only educational resources these children ever have.

We wanted to send as many school kits as we could to UMCOR. Our son Sam celebrated his ninth birthday on March 12. For his birthday party, Sam asked his friends to contribute school supplies instead of gifts. We also sent out a well-timed e-mail to Sam's uncles and aunts before a family gathering, and a few days later our $10 had grown tenfold. The grandmothers on both sides of the family are helping by making the cloth bags that will contain the school supplies.

We do not know where UMCOR will send the school kits we assemble, but we're happy just to know they're going to help kids in some corner of God's kingdom. All because of a $10 bill!

—*Cheryl, Roger, and Sam Horner*

He who is kind to the poor lends to the LORD,
and he will reward him for what he has done.
Proverbs 19:17

Honey from Heaven

WE ARE PUTTING THE $15 we received toward buying bees for our new adventure of beekeeping. We were planning to start beekeeping this summer, but we wondered what we would do with all the honey. Now we are beekeeping with a purpose. We plan to harvest the honey at the end of the summer and sell it for a donation of $50 per pound. All the proceeds will go to purchasing beehives and equipment for folks who would like to start beekeeping but cannot afford the setup, which costs about $250. Beekeeping is imperative to keep our agriculture healthy and producing. We will start with Middle Tennessee. We hope to convince the beekeeping group here in Middle Tennessee to join with us. Next, we will go statewide and then nationwide.

Kelly has been feeling a tug to do something different with her life. She has already resigned from her teaching post for next year, and we have been praying about what is next for her. This just might be it! Who knows? We are still researching the whole concept, but we feel like we can at least start small and see where it leads us.

—*Hal and Kelly Hassall*

My Story

I RECEIVED $5 AND multiplied it by having a lemonade stand. I love helping others, especially if I know someone who will be affected by my money-raising efforts. My cousin is fifteen, and he was put in a wheelchair at age thirteen. He has lost the use of his legs and most of his arm muscles, except his fine motor skills. It will eventually cause him to suffocate from the loss of his lungs. We were blessed when many people gave more than the cost of the actual lemonade. God really showed us that if we were trying to help, he would provide. I gave the money to the Muscular Dystrophy Association. It totaled $25.40!

—*Gracie Knestrick*

Pay It Forward

ON FEBRUARY 28 I picked up an envelope with $5 in it. I knew immediately where God's money was to go. I had watched an Oprah show in September, and it was on helping women around the world. I am particularly pulled toward women's issues because my husband and I have four lovely daughters. I had wanted to give to the five charities mentioned on Oprah and decided I would give to each charity at Christmas—one charity per daughter and one for me—on supporting a mom. Well, that did not happen. Who has extra money at Christmas?! So I was paying bills the Friday night before February 28, and I came across the sheet of paper listing the five charities on the Oprah show from September. Again, I kept the piece of paper on top of my bills, thinking I would try to give soon. Then at church I heard about the Living a Better Story project and its emphasis on multiplying God's money, and I knew this was God's way of showing me a better way to make an impact rather than just give my single donation. I e-mailed friends and family and asked them to go to Oprah's Web site and donate to the charity that was closest to their hearts. (Our family chose to pay for a girl to attend school for a year.) I also encouraged them to forward the link to their friends and family members and post it on their Facebook pages. Everyone has a mother, a sister, a wife, a daughter, an aunt, a cousin, or a special friend who has impacted their life. So I encouraged them to forward the link to all their e-mail contacts and make your life and someone else's a better story!

—*LeAnn Olliff Kiser and the whole Kiser family:*
Jimmy, Kelly, Jamie, Jodi, Anna Baugher, and
our son-in-law, Will Baugher

Serving Lunches
Times Two

I HAD RECENTLY SUFFERED a serious illness and had been out of church for several weeks. The first Sunday that I was able to return, the envelopes with God's money in it were passed out. As my wife and I each picked an envelope, I told her that this scared me. I realized that this was going to require action on our part because this was God's money. When we got home and opened our envelopes and each had $20 we were both reminded of the verse that says to whom much is given much is required and I wished that I had only received $5. That feeling changed as we began to pray, and by the end of the day we felt that we knew what we were being led to do. Our instructions were to pray for three days, so that is what we did. At the end of the three days our original inclination was confirmed.

Several weeks ago we saw something on television about homeless families in Nashville, so we decided to do something to help the homeless. I have a business in Brentwood that employees fourteen people. Very few of our employees bring their lunch, and most go out to get something and bring it back. Our plan was to take the Lord's $40 and provide them with homemade lunches for $8 and give the money to the Community Care Fellowship Mission downtown. We developed a handout that told the employees what we were going to do and explained that it was to multiply the loaves and fishes (God's money) by using the money given to us for supplies and offering them lunch. We both decided, however, that this was not enough. We decided that we would both do work at the mission. Shirley went last Monday to work in an after-school care center for children. I went today and I am going next week to help serve meals at lunch. We did not sell as many lunches the first week as we had hoped, but something more important has happened. Three of my employees, without being asked, want to go with me to serve lunch. I am going to take it a step at a time, but one of the things the mission needs is an older man to lead a Bible study in the afternoons for the homeless people. I will try to listen for God's direction in this as I visit weekly. I qualify in one area—I am an older man. I will need help in developing a Bible study if that is what he leads me to do. I believe that this is the start to writing a better story.

—*Gary Jackson*

Shirley's Story

WE PURCHASED FOURTEEN CHILDREN'S Bibles and distributed them Monday to the children in the Dare to Dream After School Program at Community Care Fellowship. They were so excited! We are reading the Bible stories together in our devotion each afternoon, and then they will take them with them at the end of the school year.

This has been such a rewarding and life-changing experience for both of us. Gary and four of his co-workers are serving lunches to the homeless at the center, and I am working with these precious children and loving it. We are both looking forward to helping with their Vacation Bible School in July, and we can foresee another sandwich sale next fall for another group of children in the after-school program.

—*Shirley Jackson*

Wounded Warriors

HAVE YOU EVER SAT down to pray about a specific subject after not clearing your mind in preparation to listen for what God wants to say to you? Well, that's what we thought had happened to us as we prayed about what to do with the $10 of God's money that we received in our packet. Our concentration about how to multiply and invest the money for God's people kept slipping away to another upcoming event.

On March 8 I was to be in charge of the local chapter of the National Football Foundation/College Hall of Fame awards dinner that gives fifty-three scholarships to outstanding high school football athletes from Middle Tennessee and recognizes area citizens who have distinguished themselves in various ways. What in the world did that have to do with the way we used the $10 to the glory of God? Thankfully, God works overtime to help those of us who try to make our own plan begin to discern what his plan is for us. We suddenly thought about the Fred Russell Distinguished American Award that is given at the banquet and last year's recipient, a wounded warrior—a young soldier who had been severely burned and had lost both his legs from the explosion of a roadside bomb. We thought about his courage and sacrifice as we remembered the story told that night by his commanding officer, who himself had declined the award and deferred it to this brave sergeant who was in the lead vehicle of their convoy in Iraq.

We felt God's plan coming together as we realized that instead of the awards dinner being a distraction, we could use it as an audience for growing God's money.

We collected $1,000 at the banquet in honor of a former Fred Russell Distinguished American Award recipient and have subsequently had matching gifts for an additional $2,000. On March 23, 2010, we presented $3,000 to the David Lipscomb University Wounded Warrior Program, where wounded veterans are provided a tuition-free education.

—*Robert M. Sullins*

Canines for Combat

ERE IS MY STORY about God's money. This has been a wonderful and enriching experience for me and for the others with whom I have shared the possibilities. And we are only at the beginning!

I was given $20. When we were picking up our envelopes at church, I remember having a brief hope that I would receive a smaller amount because I did not feel particularly deserving to do anything very great.

I prayed and asked for God's guidance for three days, but my answer did not come to me in a moment as a complete plan. Rather, gradually, over several days a few thoughts merged into how I could make a difference in a particular way. Here are those random thoughts that began my plan.

1. My heart aches for the many men and women serving in Iraq, Afghanistan, and other war zones. Their families suffer greatly at home, and our soldiers suffer untold losses when they are deployed and upon their return. Most do not return as the same people they were when they left. For many, their frontline injuries leave them permanently disabled.

2. My husband and I have a weekend business of selling mostly hardware at flea markets. I have added a pet supply section, and it is doing very well. Most of our customers have pets, and often our customers are veterans or have family members who are deployed, are about to be deployed, or have returned from their service.

3. A wonderful organization, the National Education for Assistance Dogs, provides trained service dogs to assist disabled persons who have suffered hearing loss, loss of mobility as a result of loss of limbs, or other disabilities. They have a special program called Canines for Combat Veterans. Established in 1976, the organization provides about fifty trained service dogs per year to disabled persons, and they train both the dogs and the people at no cost to the veteran. They receive no government funding. All their work is done through contributions from private sources and from volunteers who raise and train the dogs, veterinarians who provide medical care, and volunteers who do educational presentations for fund-raising in com-

munities across the country. Another beautiful aspect of their program is that a portion of each dog's training is accomplished through prison inmates. Participating in dog training helps prison inmates develop compassion, a sense of purpose, and an appreciation for discipline and structure. One estimate is that is costs at least $20,000 per dog prior to them.

"This has been a deeply spiritual experience because it has reminded me how important it is to listen to God instead of just talking to him."

The outcome of these puzzle pieces is that I am sending my $20, matched with $20 of my own, to Canines for Combat Veterans right away. That money will be multiplied many times over because it will assist those who volunteer their time and efforts to train the service dogs. But that is a small beginning and does not do much to provide even one service dog to a veteran. So we are adding a new line in our pet section: doggie bandanas. I have identified a source, who happens to be someone who supports animal rescue organizations with 10 percent of the profits from her business. We are going to donate 10 percent of sales proceeds from the doggie bandanas to Canines for Combat Veterans. Since I have not yet received the merchandise, you can see why I said that this is only the beginning. Although we may not raise enough to pay the full funding for a single dog, this ongoing project will help support God's work through the efforts of his many children.

Well, that is the current chapter in my story about God's money. I am very sure that God is smiling! This has been a deeply spiritual experience because it has reminded me how important it is to listen to God instead of just talking to him.

—*Dianne Glaus*

Run for Africa

HEN WE FIRST HEARD the sermon on the five loaves and two fishes in the spring, our family was inspired to use the money, multiply it, and give it back to God. We brainstormed ideas, but we finally decided to organize a group to participate with us in Ellie's Run for Africa on May 22. We asked everyone we knew to join our team, and we ended up with a dedicated group of twelve runners and walkers who were willing to join us at 7 a.m. on the first day of summer break from Ensworth High School. We used the money that was given out in church to pay our entrance fees and to bring doughnuts and coffee for motivation! In addition, we were blessed with donations from friends and relatives, all eager to help us raise as much money as possible to help give African children an education. We raised $1,700 in donations and entrance fees. Even more than that, this race was a chance for our family to bond and connect with other Nashville families, which is a huge deal to us since we recently moved here.

I thought that I understood the concept of trusting God with what I have been given and watching him multiply it beyond what I could imagine, but I've been so humbled by this experience. I guess God was determined to show me what that really meant once I put the idea to the test. What I've taken away from this experience is the realization that everything I think I understand about Christ and the way he works is only the tiniest bit of what he can offer us if we truly trust him!

—*Katherine, Don, Sandy, and Quin Cochran*

Cupcakes and Tents

WE ARE MEMBERS OF Trinity UMC in Spring Hill. My family was given $5 a few weeks ago. I have an eight-year-old son and six-year-old daughter. After discussing what we could do with them, we decided to have a cupcake stand in our driveway and use the money from these sales to purchase tents to send to Haiti. It is Haiti's rainy season, and they need temporary shelter to protect them from the relentless rain. We decided on a beautiful Saturday in March. We made signs for the end of our neighborhood, and the kids held a sign in our driveway and were very involved in flagging down people. We made forty-eight cupcakes and sold all but about ten of them. Several friends and church members came by, as well as strangers who happened to come down the street. It was a great experience. We not only turned our $5 into $118, but we also shared our story with many inquisitive customers. I went online and was able to purchase three tents to send to Haiti.

—*The Hollis Family*

Kitchen Blessings

$\mathcal{M}$Y WIFE AND I, after some thought and prayer, decided to use God's money to help his kingdom while also helping us in the process. I had been out of work for about two months at the end of last year. I was very fortunate to find a job with a good company here in Nashville. It is a small office, only seven people in addition to me. We prepared a homemade lunch for three Wednesdays in a row. I took it to the office and charged $5 per person. Through this small task that God put in front of us, we made $120. We are giving the money—along with the original $15 God gave us— to Miriam's Promise.

That in itself was great, and we both love doing God's work. What we did not expect was what happened to us over that time. Of course I told the people at the office what we were doing and why. One of the ladies there told me that she and her husband had not been to church in several years. After talking about all the great things God puts before us, she told me that last Sunday they went back to church. I was also able to tell my faith story during those lunches. My story is short, as I was baptized only six and a half years ago. It has been an incredible ride since then. Every time I tell my story, it reminds me of where I came from and where I am now. I get excited about what God has in store for me in the future.

But as for me, the most incredible thing that happened was that God brought my wife and me closer. We would spend evenings in the kitchen cooking together—no television, no radio, no distractions—just us. We would cook and laugh and clean and generally enjoy each other's company. What a wonderful blessing!

—*Ron and Pam Patterson*

Blog for Bears

MY SEVEN-YEAR-OLD daughter received $5 in her envelope at church. We are working together as a family to try to raise $560 to send teddy bears to all the children in the Raining Season orphanage in Sierra Leone. So far we have raised over $240 by running a lemonade stand and using Facebook. We even started a blog, teddybearsforsierraleone.blogspot.com, for friends to link to their blog. My daughter's dance teacher is helping us by providing her Noah's Ark Animal Workshop so Sarah and her friends can stuff the teddy bears themselves. Her dance teacher is contributing five of the bears from her family and all the stuffing, certificates, and necklaces that go with the bears. It's great to see Sarah and our family working so hard for this fun, worthwhile project!

—*Holly Fisher*

Remembering Dad

*M*ANY PEOPLE AND EVENTS influence our lives and become part of the story we live. While trying to develop our plan for the cash we received in the Living a Better Story kit, my wife and I began thinking of influences on our stories and ways to honor them as we made our decision. Brenda began talking about my father, G. W. Eddlemon, and the life he had lived. A devoutly Christian man, he was the most gentle and peaceful man you could ever meet. He loved his family, friends, church, and most of all God. He was not one for long conversations, but his words and actions had more meaning than anyone I have ever known.

These qualities that everyone who knew my father appreciated are even more profound by knowing his story. In the early months of 1942, while serving with the U.S. Army Air Corps in the Philippines, his unit was captured by the Japanese army. They were banded together with all the other captured U.S. and Filipino troops in the southern Bataan Peninsula and began a six-day, seventy-mile journey that became known as the Bataan Death March. Starvation and beatings resulted in the deaths of thousands and thousands of soldiers. Those who survived spent the next three and a half years in prisoner-of-war camps in the Philippines and in Japan.

My father kept most of his memories locked inside, offering only a few glimpses to those of us on the outside. But in the 1980s he began to release more and more details. As he did, he would talk about the Filipinos and the risk they took to offer food and water to the soldiers along the march. Many of them were killed for their acts of kindness to the soldiers. Whenever Dad talked about his experiences, he would always say that only by the grace of God did he survive. He passed away a few years ago, but his life is an inspiration to us as we strive to Live a Better Story.

In honor of my father, we increased the amount received to $25 and used this to participate in a micro-loan program. Our money was added to other contributors from around the world to fund a loan for a Filipino fisherman who makes his living by selling his catch. My dad loved to fish. The loan will help this family have a better life. Once the loan is repaid, it will be rolled into another loan, and the cycle will continue. We will use my dad's inspiration as we each try to Live a Better Story, and our prayer is that this small amount of seed money will help change the lives of many people for years to come.

—*Tom and Brenda Eddlemon*

Seeds of Love

WANT TO SHARE some thoughts about Living a Better Story. On February 22, I took a friend out for lunch and gave her a gift card for her birthday. This friend is a single mom (a church member) who has been struggling financially for several years and is three months behind on her mortgage payment. While there is little I can do to help with that, I can listen and encourage her.

I spent my $5 and David's $5 on $16 worth of much-needed items for Graceworks Pantry. Simply adding money to that which was given to us is not very creative, but I had read about this need in the newspaper and felt led to do this.

Sunday afternoon I visited two friends (also from church) who are recovering from an extended illness and a recent surgery. I took each of them a pot of tulips to cheer them (thinking it would cheer me if I were bedridden) and visited with them for a few minutes. No money involved, just time, and we all benefited.

I find that if I am listening and watching, God will let me hear about some needs, and I have learned to respond to them. I always regret it if I do not listen and follow.

Living a Better Story has united the people of our church and has people excited about the endless possibilities. Thanks be to God. All things are possible with God!

—*Linda Troutman*

Open Doors

MY WIFE MERRILY AND I are facilitating one of the small groups that meet at 11:00 a.m. on Sundays. It has been a great experience for both of us, and we have thoroughly enjoyed it. Our group decided that we would work together to put to use the money we received in the Living a Better Story envelopes. We decided to help one of Merrily's patients: a young man with a severe neuromuscular disease. While he is intellectually fine, he cannot walk, talk, or communicate in any way. As you can imagine, he is very depressed. He is in a nursing home in Lewisburg. A special type of computer is available that would allow him to communicate and even use the Internet, but unfortunately, his family does not have the means, and his insurance does not cover such equipment. Our group's original intent was to raise some seed money for this device, which will cost between $4,000 and $5,000. One of our members reached out to some of his business contacts, and we have already received over $4,000. This has been amazing and truly shows all of us the doors God opens when we focus on what we can do for others.

—David Jones

The Stillness Is God

'VE ALWAYS CONSIDERED MYSELF a spiritual person, never once questioning the path God has planned for me. However, while sitting by the fire and reading Donald Miller's *A Million Miles in a Thousand Years*, I remembered a sermon by my childhood preacher, Brother Donnie, in which he said, "When we are with other people, they should be able to see Jesus's love in our faces, and should feel his compassion and concern in our hands." I wondered, What do people see when they look at me? Do they see Jesus's love in my face? Do they feel his compassion and concern in my touch? I thought for a moment. How could they? Because seeking daily guidance from the Holy Spirit was at the very bottom of my to-do list. I was so lost I could not follow the bread crumbs back to the path of salvation because I was not living God's story. I was simply ignoring God's voice.

This was my aha! moment. I was ready to get busy and trust in God so I could begin to live a better story, a story worth talking about. Then the phone rang. It was my parents calling from Texas with devastating news. I could hear the fear in my mom's voice when she quietly said, "My preliminary lung biopsy was not good. The doctors think there's a chance I may have cancer." Hours after hanging up the phone, those vicious words kept ringing in my head. I felt the ground beneath me shifting, shaking me to my knees, not to pray, but to selfishly scream at God, "I decided to trust in you. Why are you doing this?"

Throughout the following week I was angry at God, kicking and screaming like a defiant two-year-old having a temper tantrum. Looking back, all I really wanted was for someone to lend me a hand, tell me everything was going to be okay, and pick me up off the floor. As the week went on, feelings of sadness and loneliness mounted as I struggled with the reality of my mom's diagnosis.

As I sat in church the following Sunday and listened to Reverend Cliff's sermon, suddenly an almost eerie calm came over me. I stopped screaming inside. I sat there for a moment, trying not to breathe, in awe, and I realized this was exactly what I had asked for earlier in the week. It was God, whispering in my ear, "I am here. You are not alone." This truly is the meaning of "Ask, and it shall be given...seek, and ye shall find." This was a life-changing experience for me. One thing I know for sure is that when you shift your paradigm to what you can do for others, you begin to accelerate your own evolution and trigger a bounty of blessings. That moment is always available to us. If you peel back the layers of your life—the frenzy, the noise— stillness is waiting. That stillness is God!

P.S. My mom had a bronchoscopy and a second CT-guided lung biopsy last week, and the results were good news! The doctors are going to monitor the suspicious spot for now. They are not convinced that it is cancer. Hallelujah!

As an update on what I'm doing with God's money: My father served as a volunteer fireman for over thirty years at the community fire station. They have agreed to donate all the money raised at the annual pancake supper to lung cancer research. Wow! What a blessing!

—*Melissa James*

A Red Wagon Full

OR MY LIVING A BETTER STORY EXPERIENCE, I collected $230 plus our family's $35, which I used to buy newly released DVDs. I also received 211 new and previously viewed DVDs. In total, several weeks ago I took 229 DVDs plus several boxes of comics that a fellow Boy Scout in my troop donated to Vanderbilt University Children's Hospital. Mom and I had so many DVDs and comics that it took a rolling duffle bag, two large shopping bags, and one of the hospital's red wagons to bring the full load into the hospital. I had the chance to tell head volunteer about my church and the Living a Better Story project. She was very impressed. Since my visit, I have collected an additional 139 DVDs. I will be taking those when I go for my next appointment. Thanks to all of the friends who supported me, I was able to multiply our family's original $35 and give way more than I thought possible.

—*Ben Watson*

Investing in Goodness

A T THE BEGINNING OF the Living a Better Story experience, we were asked to report back in three weeks to let the church know how we had multiplied and invested God's money. So the best way to sum up where we are is to say that we are on the road. This experience has further enhanced conversations that Dirk and I had been having last year and more intently at the start of this year when the Living a Better Story sermons began. We have three young children, and so we realized that we had a great opportunity and desire to do more with our lives and set a good example in the process for them. We decided to start a giving investment club. This was not a typical playing-the-stocks club, but more of a pooling of money, talents, and resources to make a difference in the world as a family. At the moment, there are three other families that have made an initial commitment to the club. Our plan is not to make this a one-time chance to help others but truly create a lifestyle of generosity. We are not yet sure where this will lead us, and we are still praying about specific ways to use God's money. But as a community of families, we will be accountable to each other in prayer and presence as Christ's hands and feet. In a nutshell, we are investing in each other so that we as a group can invest in others to make them desire to invest their own gifts and talents to make this world a better place. *To be continued ...*

—*Rachael Melton*

Dinner Party for Parkinson's

I DID NOT KNOW at that time how much money our dinner party would raise, but it turned out to be $430. After the dinner party, I contacted the Parkinson's Disease Foundation to be sure the donation was submitted properly. The lady who returned my call wanted to know more about why Sonny and I chose to host this event. I shared with her the Living a Better Story project at BUMC. She was very impressed and, just as we had done, related it to the movie *Pay It Forward*. The foundation was most appreciative and stated that, due to the economy, their donations were really down. It was a wonderful experience. When the party gathered for a prayer prior to dinner, I felt very emotional.

—*Sonny and Elaine Kolaks*

Friends of Sadie

SADIE WAS A THERAPY dog that visited nursing homes and shared her sweet spirit and wagging tail with everyone. The nursing home patients thoroughly enjoyed Sadie's visits. She learned the paws-up command, putting her paws on the patients' beds or laps so she could be petted. Visiting patients is stressful for a dog, but Sadie went about her work with a calm and a joy that was a pleasure to watch. Sadie was a wonderful dog, and all who met her recognized her loving spirit and loved her in return. When we were given the opportunity to Live a Better Story, and after we had received our money from the church and prayed for three days to see where God would lead us to multiply the money, I felt God leading me to use the money to make a donation in Sadie's memory to the therapy group of which she was a part. We all love animals in our family and realize how much they can brighten anyone's day. Our family was in agreement that this was where God was leading us. We sent an e-mail to family and friends and asked them to make a donation to Therapy Dogs International in sweet Sadie's memory.

—*Carol Demumbrum*

A Little Can Go a Long Way

ON THE SUNDAY WHEN the packets were passed out, I was very excited about this special initiative and knew right away what I thought we should do. Between me, my husband, and our two children, we had a total of $40. My employer was winding down a monthlong Haiti relief matching donation fund-raiser through which we matched dollar for dollar our team members' donations to Haiti relief. It felt good about being able to double the donation, and I kicked in $60 more so that the combined $100 donation would be doubled to $200.

Having given some thought to how blessed we are and how what may not seem like a lot of money to us can actually go a long way in helping others, my daughter Lindsay and I decided to make a donation to the Heifer Foundation, whose mission is to partner with people in a global movement to end hunger and poverty and care for the earth. Their simple belief is that ending hunger begins with giving people the means to feed themselves. Since 1944 Heifer has helped more than 10.5 million hungry families in the United States and 125 other countries move toward self-reliance through the gift of food and income-producing animals. Lindsay and I enjoyed looking at the available options to donate livestock and discussing how different animals could help a family be more self-sustaining. We ultimately decided that a goat would be a practical choice because a family could produce milk for their own use or to take it to market. Since then I have occasionally framed things we've bought in comparison to how many goats we could have bought with the money, which serves as a reminder that we are blessed and how far that money could go toward helping others.

We were happy to make the Haiti relief donation and the Heifer Foundation donation, but after hearing the stories of what others have done, our efforts feel inadequate and insignificant in the scheme of things, like we took an easy route. The stories have been inspiring though and have caused us to think about how we can use our talents and gifts to help others. It's exciting to see the impact of the anonymous donation and what we have been challenged to do.

—*The Latto Family: Greg, Nada,*
  Daniel, and Lindsay

Laundry Basket Epiphany

AFTER PRAYING AND BEING patient about what to do with my Living a Better Story investment, my answer came this last week. I was lamenting over folding my third basket of clean clothes one night. I have three children, all of which are involved in sports, so you can imagine how many loads of laundry I do weekly. After folding the last basket for the night, I checked my third grader's school folder and found the flyer advertising our semiannual clothing drive this week for our sister school, Schwab Elementary, in Nashville. At Schwab, 85 percent of the families live below the poverty level. Once in the fall and once in the spring, we donate gently worn clothes that our kids have outgrown and pass them on to this elementary school, where the children are elated to receive "new" clothes. At the bottom of the flyer was a request for packages of new underwear for the kids who did not have any.

Wow! It hit me like a ton of bricks. How selfish could I be by getting frustrated with the amount of laundry I have to do at my house every day. Not only do my kids have ample underwear, they have the luxury to choose styles of underwear. At that moment, I knew my $10 would be buying new underwear for a Schwab Elementary student. I shared the information from the flyer with my nine-year-old, and he quickly decided that his charity savings would be used for the same purpose. We have always required our kids to put aside 25 percent of their weekly allowance to be used for the charity of their choice. When Reed checked his charity jar, he had $11. So the $10 in my envelope has become $21 to buy new underwear for some elementary school kids who do not have enough. What a great exercise! It helped put the story I'm living in perspective for me.

—*Mary Massengale*

Children's Art for Children's Health

MY ENVELOPE HAD $20. My son Jackson's envelope had $5. My sister Julie McKim's envelope had $5. We've decided to use our combined $30 to fund an art sale. (This actually came from an idea Jackson had a while back to "sell paintings to make money for sick children in the hospital." He loves making art.) We've been to the art store to buy paper, pastel oils, and charcoals, and I've talked with Kinko's about producing eight-by-ten copies. Tomorrow night my sister and her family are coming over so we can eat together before creating the paintings. The plan is to have Jackson, Mason, and my nephew Maddox each create an original picture. We are then going to e-mail the images to as many friends and family members as we can, explain the church-wide initiative, tell our story, and take orders for reprints. (We're still working out the final price point; we're thinking between $15 and $20 per print.) We are also thinking about posting the story on each of our Facebook accounts to help spread the word and hopefully generate more sales. We allowed Jackson to pick the charity for which we are raising funds. He picked St. Jude's. His goal is to sell twenty prints. I have faith that we will surpass that.

—*Michele Peden*

God's Different Plan

$\mathcal{M}$Y SISTER PASSED AWAY on July 17, 2009 in her sleep. No illness, no warning. It devastated me. She was my only sister and my only living female relative. Growing up, Linda was dependent on me for financial assistance. She never graduated school or held a full-time job. I helped with her bills until we had to make some tough-love decisions. I stopped enabling her, but I would never let her go hungry or lack electricity or be cold. That continued pretty much all my adult life.

After she passed away, I missed her monthly phone calls for help. I wanted to start a nonprofit organization to assist those who cannot pay their utility bills. When this envelope was handed to me, I received $10. I thought, "Great! I can start my dream of helping those without the resources to pay their utility bills." Well, God had a different plan.

I prayed and prayed about it. It did not come easy. During that first week of prayer, I received word that a co-worker's sister was very sick and had been hospitalized. My friend has been traveling back and forth to Alabama to visit his sick sister and take care of his elderly mother. It has weighed him down financially and emotionally. His sister was put on life support last week. While he and his mother were at the hospital, the mother's house burned to the ground. The sister's house was adjacent to the mother's house. *Both burned to the ground!* They lost everything, including both of their dogs and one cat. The mother lost all her medication, which she could not afford to replace immediately. They were underinsured, and despite all the red tape, she needed this medication immediately.

I took God's $10 and prayed that we could collect enough money at the office to send to this friend and his mother to help them get through the week, or until the insurance was able to begin to cover their loss. Even though I had nothing to do with the collection at the office, I did send him $310 (God's $10 and an additional $300) to help with a couple of nights of hotel accommodations, but most important, to pay for his mother's medications. I know God will bless those people because great prayer is upon them. Our heavenly Father watches over them and has already blessed me by knowing them.

—*Cheryl Ballesteros*

Dearest Lord, teach me to be generous;

Teach me to serve you as you deserve;

To give and not to count the cost,

To fight and not to seek for rest,

To labor and not to seek reward,

Save that of knowing that I do your will.

—St. Ignatius Of Loyola

Turning on Hope

ATTENDED YOUR CHURCH on the Wednesday night after the Sunday that the $25,000 was distributed. I think there were 180 packets left, and I took one. I had been invited by a friend to attend the Wednesday night service on the study of the Book of Revelation.

I found $5 in my packet. As directed, I prayed for three days, and then I took the $5 and turned it into five one-dollar bills. Each one-dollar bill represented one person. Now, I had five people to help. I had a gift certificate from Barnes and Nobles. I bought four Bibles and contributed one of my own. I now had five Bibles.

I often pass the Nashville Electric Service building on Church Street in Nashville and see many poor people waiting in line in the cold to pay their bill to keep their electricity from being disconnected. I knew I was to pay for five people's bills, but I did not know quite how to do it.

I prayed all the time I was driving to NES. I went in and saw two men sitting at a help desk. I told them I wanted to pay for five people's electric bills. I told them I was doing the Lord's work. They were stunned and then thanked me for what I was doing. They directed me to an assistant. I told her my story. She was stunned and then smiled and called her supervisor. I again told my story. I said that I wanted to pay five people's electric bills up to $500 each. She had a list of people in dire need of help with their bills. I told her the only stipulation was that each of the five people also would receive a Bible. We then started the process of paying for each one. I now have reached five people at NES. She gave me the name of the person whose bill I was paying, and I wrote in each of the five Bibles the person's name, that the gift was from God, and that God loved them. I wrote in the date: March 16, 2010.

My feeling about this experience is one of tremendous gratitude to God who has so richly blessed me. Many years ago, when I was a single mom with three children, my electricity was turned off because I could not pay the bill. I will never forget that horrible feeling. To think that I was able to pay $2,165.55 for someone else's electric bills makes me shake my head in wonder at the awesomeness of God.

—*Edna Holland*

This is what the LORD says:
"Let not the wise man boast of his wisdom
or the strong man boast of his strength
or the rich man boast of his riches,
but let him who boasts boast about this:
that he understands and knows me,
that I am the LORD, who exercises kindness,
justice and righteousness on earth,
for in these I delight,"
declares the LORD.
Jeremiah 9:22-24

God's Call to Act for Others

SEVERAL MONTHS AGO, MY wife and I attended Brentwood United Methodist Church while visiting some friends in Brentwood. It was that Sunday when the congregation was surprised with the cash distributions! We were deeply moved by your challenge to pass along the money in Jesus's name. God has blessed us greatly during these challenging economic times, unlike so many of our neighbors and church friends. We both knew that the Lord was calling us to act on his behalf for the benefit of others, but the scope of the need around us had frozen us as to what to do and in what amount.

The $10 we received from you that Sunday many weeks ago was the catalyst for us to act to help some friends who had been unemployed for more than a year. We passed along your $10, plus $2,990 of our own, to these friends anonymously, but in God's name. We are grateful for this challenge. It helped us to see exactly how God was calling us.

—*Grateful Visitors*

A Time to Listen to God

MY NAME IS Rachel Gwinn, and I, along with Janet Ross, attend BUMC on a regular basis. We were both lucky enough to be a part of the Living a Better Story series and received envelopes to multiply God's money. We decided to put our money together, and it totaled $25.

After prayerful consideration, we chose the following three ways to multiply the money:

We made a Cuss Bucket and placed $1 in it each time we said a negative word.

We challenged ten of our closest friends to do the same for a full week.

We used our $25 to have a spaghetti dinner for all twelve who participated. Donations were also taken for the meal, and we actually fed everyone and stayed within the $25 budget.

After collecting the bucket money and the donations for dinner, we had $502. This money was donated to Graceworks Ministries in Franklin and earmarked for senior citizens who need some assistance with their utility bills.

We were so thrilled to be a part of such a great project and share it with our friends. The first three days were definitely challenging, because we wanted to brainstorm immediately. The three days of prayer, however, were a time to listen to God. By the way, most of the money came from donations for dinner!

—*Rachel Gwinn*

Jumping for Joy

 Y TWELVE-YEAR-OLD daughter Claire and I were at the service where
the Living a Better Story packets were handed out. She received $5
and I received $10. As soon as Cliff started talking about what to do with
the money, I knew what I wanted to do. On the way home from church I
asked Claire if she knew what she wanted to do with the money, and right
away, she said, "Yes!" I asked her what her idea was, and it was the same as
mine. That was the first sign that I knew God was pointing us in the right
direction. We agreed to pray about it for three days, and during that time I
asked God to show us how to increase our money so we could accomplish
our project.

Because my daughter is in the sixth grade, she is presently attending
confirmation classes. One of their requirements is to do a community project. After much prayer, we decided to involve her best friend, Emily Stad-
nick, who is also attending confirmation classes. I am Emily's friend-in-faith
and Emily's mother, Tracy, is Claire's friend-in-faith. We got together and
asked them if they would like to be a part of our Living a Better Story project, and they agreed. We brainstormed and decided on a project that would
be a good confirmation project, involve the community, and help one of our
neighbors who is going through a very tough time.

Our project was to host a benefit at Pump It Up, an establishment
owned by a BUMC member who also helped make this project possible. At
Pump It Up, the rooms are filled with inflatables, slides, and a rock-
climbing wall, along with great music playing overhead. Because the ca-
pacity of the facility is 110, we decided to make it a girls-only event. Our
girls came up with a "Girls Night Out" theme where they could wear their
PJs, jump for an hour, and socialize. Instead of paying to attend, we asked
for monetary donations to help our neighbor who has cancer. We wanted
to raise some money to help cover some of her costs that were not covered
by insurance.

Time was of the essence. Our neighbor had three weeks until her radiation started. She had already spent weeks in chemotherapy, and we only had one week until our event. We created a flyer to send out as an invitation. We decided to print one hundred copies because half would go to the confirmation class of girls and leaders. The rest of the copies would go to school friends and neighborhood girls. When I went to Office Depot to make the copies, I took my $15 from the church. The total cost to make the copies was $14.14. Was God present or what?

With the invitations out, we were ready. We hosted our event last Friday night. The girls made a donation box and greeted everyone as they came in the door. Everyone was so generous. We turned our $15 into more than $500 for our sweet neighbor. My heart swells because it is filled with God's love. He has revealed himself not only to me but to my daughter, her best friend, and to the multitude of people who were involved in this project, including my dear, sweet husband who had to stand in for me on Friday night and was the only guy in the presence of many screaming twelve-year-olds. What a man!

Sunday we will present the money to our neighbor. I am sure she will be overwhelmed not only by the money but by the total love and support these girls have given out of the goodness of their hearts.

—*Kris Sager*

God Likes Good Coffee, Too

WE WERE VISITING Brentwood United Methodist Church on the Sunday when the money was given to the congregation to Live a Better Story. We received $5 and used it to purchase some coffee from Harvest Hands. Returning to our new home in Fairfield Glade, Norm served it to the Fairfield Glade UMC Men's Club and explained the Humphreys Street Coffee program. It was suggested that we purchase coffee in large quantities in order to use their bulk sale price list and resell it as our own fund-raiser. The men's club has agreed to do this and also wants to present the coffee to our 950-member congregation to purchase. Not only will this help Harvest Hands on the front end, but the profits we generate at resale will help to support the outreach and mission projects of the FGUMC Men's Club. A win-win situation. Opportunities for going farther into the community are unlimited as we see where else God leads us. I guess even God likes a good cup of coffee!

—*Norm and Linda Anderson*

Loose Change and Patience

RECEIVED $5 and multiplied it to $75. I did not have much time to be creative. It started multiplying when I told friends what Brentwood UMC was doing, and everyone said, "I will match your $5 or give $1." When I was helping my parents in Kentucky, all my siblings came for Sunday lunch and I told them what BUMC was doing and I collected a few more dollars. Whenever I find money—even a penny—I will pick it up and bring it home and put it in a container. I do not spend money that I find, but I save it until I find a good place to put it. My container had about $10 in it. That was added to God's money. When I went out to eat, I ordered just a sandwich instead of a meal and placed the difference in the money pot.

Honestly, after three days of asking God what I should do with his money, I was not getting a clear picture. I had convinced myself that I would put it into a couple of church outreach programs, but I did not have a positive feeling that I should do that, because I do that anyway. When I was down to my last week, I said, "God I need to know if I am making the right decision with your money." This past Monday morning, the first thing that hit me was a thought about my son's friends in Georgia. The father had lost his job last year. My money is going to this young family in Georgia.

—*S. Hubbard*

To Russia with Love

WE WERE NOT IN church on the Sunday the Living a Better Story envelopes were passed out. The first Sunday after returning from Florida, it was the buzz going around the church. Mary Lou and I realized we have been living a better story the last four years.

After returning from Russia six years ago, we realized we wanted to help the Russian church. We had attended a church service when we were there, and the congregation was so loving and had so little that we wanted to help them. After the church service, which lasted between two and three hours, they share a meal, because some of them have to travel an hour or two to get home. In 2006 we heard that they were going to build a kitchen in the church. The members could then travel to their homes after a warm meal.

Marv's hobby is photography, but he had never used it except for his own pleasure. He realized he could use his pictures of flowers to make note cards, sell them, and give that money to the Russian church to help pay for the kitchen. He also made and sold desk calendars. The first year, we made over $1,500, which was given to the Russian church for the kitchen.

Since that time Mary Lou has been knitting dishcloths, and I have been taking more pictures of our church and making calendars and note cards. To date we have given money to the Russian church, a school in South Africa, and Harvest Hands.

—*Marv and Mary Lou Bartels*

Sharing the Wealth

WE RECEIVED TWO Living a Better Story packets from BUMC member and friend, Lorrie Brouse. The total amount we received was $15. A couple of days later, we saw a grocery store flyer coupon that offered a huge discount on breakfast cereal. The maximum that could be purchased at any one time was five boxes. We thought we could use the money to buy cereal for the pantry operated by our local church. But first we started collecting flyers. With our multiple flyers, we kept going back to the store over and over until the offer expired. We never did get around to using the $15—it simply provided the seed money for all our cereal purchases. Now we've found a similar deal on soup, and we're going to keep the process going. We've been saying we'll just give the $15 to the pantry along with the food, but we may hang on to it because it reminds us to share out of our wealth to help others. Thanks for helping us to partner with God in this way.

—*Tom and Laura Rothhaar*

Giving Back

I T HAS BEEN A LONG TIME since I have been able to give a gift to someone else. For the past year and a half, I have relied on the charity of others. I am grateful for the gifts given to me by the church, local career support agencies, and my family. However, I could not give back to a society that had given to me. It brings me great happiness to be able to give now. It is not much, this donation, but it has given me a chance to give when I thought I could not.

I have given the money to the students at the Wesley Foundation at the University of Virginia. I have always wanted to give to the religious group I was a part of in college. It is a joy to be able to give when I thought I could not. I hope they use the money for worship or a hearty, homemade dinner for the students.

—*John and Kimberly Wade*

Back to the Praying Board

I WOULD LIKE TO SUBMIT my "so-far" story. Like a lot of other stories, I have struggled with this task. I have had several ideas, but none have really stuck. I guess the hardest part is coming up with an idea and then realizing I am looking at a ten-dollar bill. (I know, my mind is in a box.)

So after work one day, I went to a Christian bookstore to get some cards to send to my family. The nice lady at the counter asked if I would be interested in buying a Bible. She showed me a really nice Bible. She then told me it was only $5. I remembered my mom needed a new Bible, so I said sure. Then she asked me if I had ever heard of the Christian Women's Job Corps of Middle Tennessee. I said no. She told me a little about it and showed me a box on the back counter where they were collecting donations for these $5 Bibles. Then I had an idea. My wife received $5 for her Living a Better Story money, so I called her, but she was in the middle of something.

After I got off the phone, I realized that I could do something with my money. So I multiplied my $10 by ten, and I was able to buy twenty-two Bibles for only $110. At first I thought this was a great story, and then I realized that I had only multiplied God's money with my money. I really did not think out of the box or get anyone else involved. So I have decided go back to the praying board.

—*Nahshon Roth*

A Guardian Angel?

I received $10 of God's money during the Living a Better Story experience. I multiplied that to $415.30 through the purchase of numerous household items from Costco, which I then handdelivered to Graceworks.

While making the delivery, I observed a young lady filling out some paperwork in the waiting room. I inquired about her and was told she was there for some assistance. Her truck was parked near mine. When she started to leave, I approached her and asked if she needed further assistance. She broke down crying and declined my offer, telling me how difficult it was for her to seek help. She said she had broken her wrist and could not work, and her husband had recently abandoned her and her two daughters. I told her I would like to help her and asked her to follow me to Sam's, where she could pick out some things. After considerable persuasion she reluctantly followed me.

She was very grateful as she picked up some things and could not believe her good fortune. She was hesitant about picking up anything as we went through the store, though. I told her to look at this as if it were Christmas. She told me this was better than Christmas and expressed her gratitude repeatedly. The receipt at Sam's totaled $397.15. I told her to view that as bread cast on the water, and when she could, she could pass on the blessing to another. She said she definitely would.

I prefer personal contributions whenever I can, as it gives me a chance to pass on God's love directly to another of his children. She asked me if I just hung around places looking for people to help. I told her no, that she just happened to be at the right place at the right time to get a small dose of help that keeps on going.

She and I both wondered for a moment if maybe I was a guardian angel. I know I'm not, but I am trying to stay in contact with her to see if I can help her through the maze of difficulties she faces. Her greeting on her voicemail concludes with "Have a blessed day." For that one day, I believe I blessed her, and it felt good. Thanks for giving me the impetus to help one of God's children.

—*Richard G. Knudsen*

Therefore do not worry, saying, "What will we eat?" or
"What will we drink?" or "What will we wear?" For it is the Gentiles
who strive for all these things; and indeed your heavenly Father knows that
you need all these things. But strive first for the kingdom of God and his
righteousness, and all these things will be given to you as well.
Matthew 6:31-33

Impact Locally and Joyfully

W E PLAN ON STARTING a scholarship fund at the high school where Hal teaches and coaches in order to give away an annual scholarship to a deserving senior boys basketball player. It will be named in honor and memory of Hal's late father, who was a basketball coach, too. There is so much need right under our noses that we do not see because of all of the international news and tragedy. I know those people are needy, but we feel like we can have an impact locally, and our hearts would be just as full of joy. As with anything, there will be obstacles to overcome in raising this money, but this is speaking to our hearts, and we really want to do it.

—*Hal and Holly Murrell*

Red Carpet Blessings

WE WOULD LIKE TO thank the person who donated the money that made it possible for us to Live a Better Story. There are four of us who sit on the same pew almost every Sunday and Wednesday night, and we went together on this journey.

The Oscars were coming up, and we decided it was a good reason for a party. Donations would be accepted as tickets. The sidewalk and steps were lit up to show off the red carpet. There were lighted banners on the house, along with an official Oscar poster, and guests arrived in red-carpet attire. There was plenty of food and drink, statuettes sitting around, and even ballots on which to vote for who you thought would win. A golden egg would go to the guest with the most correct votes. But the highlight of the evening was the reason for it all—to help children in the area dress for school. Twenty-five dollars will buy two pairs of pants, two shirts, socks, and a belt. The Assistance League of Nashville does all of this and so much more. They buy books and help children in need.

Our $40 grew like the loaves and fishes to $600, which will help so many children, but not nearly as much as it helped us. Among the blessings that night were our many friends who were touched by the stories of living a better life and blessed us with their support.

—*Patricia Hoover*

God's Silly String

I WAS EXCITED ABOUT this challenge. I knew that we were supposed to pray about what to do with the money for three days, but an idea came into my head the moment Reverend Wright started to explain the challenge. My idea was to hold a small bike ride for the neighborhood kids and ask for donations for Dylan Young.

Dylan attends kindergarten at Crockett Elementary. Shortly before Thanksgiving, Crockett Elementary sponsored "Dollars for Dylan." Dylan and his family traveled to Boston for a life-saving surgery for Dylan. Crockett students raised a good portion of the money needed, but I suspect that it was not enough.

My son, Thomas, was on board immediately. He printed up flyers and distributed them to all of his friends. After the race, the contestants would get to play with Silly String in the front yard.

I took the $10 and bought ten cans of Silly String. I am pretty sure this was the first time God has ever bought Silly String. I contacted Dylan's father, and he was very excited about the idea. He wanted Dylan to participate. He wrote a very nice e-mail about how fortunate his family was to have the support of the entire community.

"I learned that doubt is going to be a part of Living a Better Story, but it will all work out with God in charge."

Everything was going well until doubt started to set in. The weather report called for rain, I had not received the e-mail finalizing plans with Dylan's father, and it was against school policy to send home the flyers we had made. I prayed. I asked my Sunday school class to pray for good weather.

The race was Friday afternoon, and the weather was spectacular. Dylan was sick and could not attend, but he wished us all well. We rounded up eleven kids and rode our bikes. Then the winners sprayed Silly String all over each other, laughter was heard, and it was beautiful. We raised $90, and more donations are coming in.

I learned that doubt is going to be a part of Living a Better Story, but it will all work out with God in charge.

—*Lisa Abramson*

Encouragement in the Grass

I MUST START BY saying how completely blessed I was by this opportunity. I happened to be back in Nashville for the weekend (I attended BUMC when I lived in Brentwood four years ago), and attending the service on February 21 was probably the best part of my trip. I received an unexpected $30 gift card from work a few days after the $10 I received at BUMC that Sunday. Realizing that none of this money was expected or deserved, I pooled it and set out to spend all $40 on the project. The Dollar General down the street from my house was relocating (they're closed now), so with my $40 budget, I was able to get several lawn ornaments, which I gave to my grandmother's retirement home in South Georgia. Not only will they serve to bless the residents and the workers there, but also those of us who visit there. I delivered the ornaments this past Tuesday during my trip home, and the owners, Raymond and Kaye, could not have been more appreciative. By the time I left to come back to Atlanta on Thursday, Kaye had dispersed the ornaments throughout the property (it's a twelve-room facility), but I did not take pictures, because I told her I did not want any of the glory to go to me but to God above. I showed her the Living a Better Story literature, and she understood completely where I was coming from.

I've been very lacking in my volunteer and donation activities as of late, and this has not only encouraged me to become involved with charity work again, but to also use what God's given me for his glory and honor every single day.

—*Brian Tucker*

Lemonade Stand for God

I RECEIVED $5 AND my husband Mark received $10. We both thought a lot about how to multiply the money. After praying about it for about a week, we realized that we would involve our grandchildren and have a lemonade stand. We have five grandchildren—a five-year-old, two two-year-olds, a one-year-old, and a seven-month-old. I took our five-year-old granddaughter to the grocery store, and she decided to buy lemonade, doughnuts, and peanuts. We made a sign, and they all helped to decorate it. We set it up in front of her house, and all five grandchildren helped to flag down customers, sell, and pour the lemonade. They did manage to eat up a lot of the profits, but they really got into it and were excited to give the money to God. We chose to give our money to The Next Door, a prison ministry for women. I love being a member of such a wonderful church and hope to Live a Better Story each and every day.

—*Ann and Mark Nussmeyer*

Lessons in Miracles

SUNDAY MORNING, February 21, I was surprised to feel a special nudge from the Holy Spirit to go to church. For many months, due to health reasons, I had been unable to attend. I am so glad I paid attention to the nudge, for now I know that God had a beautiful lesson in miracles for me.

During the service I was delighted to hear about the Living a Better Story series. I found myself feeling both amazed and grateful to be a member of a church that wants to put action to its words. I was especially delighted to be invited to take an envelope with a small investment of God's money so that I, too, could experience what it means to Live a Better Story.

As I opened my envelope and found $10, I felt many of the same feelings the disciples expressed when told to feed the five thousand with five loaves and two fishes: confusion, doubt, and inadequacy. Like me, they lacked the faith to believe that Jesus could take what little they had and turn it into even more than they could possibly imagine. Thankfully, all my concerns were addressed in church through the literature and a video presentation. I realized that it was not my responsibility to perform the miracle but simply to pray, listen, and trust God with the outcome and the story.

What a great lesson and journey to sit quietly and wait on God to reveal his plan for investing his money. As I prayed and listened, I have to admit doubts still arose, but I was willing to give it a try. Thankfully, I did not have to wait long. I knew by the fourth day what I was to do. I got so excited thinking about the answer that I could not help imagining how joyful the recipient would be.

A dear friend of mine is the outreach director for Faith Family Medical Clinic, one of the ministries our church supports. It provides faith-based healthcare to the working uninsured. She had been trying to book me for several months to do a team-building workshop. Her hope was that it would help them offer even better patient care to those who cannot afford it.

During my prayer time, God impressed upon me to use the $10 for some of my materials for the workshop and to offer my $500 fee as an in-kind contribution to her and the clinic, thus multiplying His money fifty times! She was both humbled and thrilled with the story and God's continued care for their work. She said, "Think of the ripple effect this will have to the rest of the staff and the patients."

It was a true miracle that day that Jesus took five loaves and two fishes, blessed them, and fed over five thousand hungry people. For me, however, the greater miracle that took place that day was that Jesus took the time to invite his beloved imperfect disciples to join him in making the miracle happen. The good news is that he is still inviting beloved, imperfect disciples like me to join him in making miracles happen today!

—*Marlane Peak*

Living a Better Story
at the Masters

I T IS TOTALLY A GOD THING that my friend Edna and I got to go to the Masters in the first place. We went Thursday through Sunday, not the practice rounds—the real tournament. Maybe it was because we needed to live out a part of our Better Story there. You know, we should never limit God.

While driving to Augusta, we decided that we would take a taxi or shuttle to the course rather than try to drive, since this was our first time and we had no idea where we were to go. As we walked across the parking lot to check into the hotel, we spotted a young man beside a van with "Short Cut Shuttle" on its side. As we got closer, I could see that his shirt said, "Crossroad Church Global Missions." We asked if this was his van. He began to explain that during Masters week the church runs shuttles to the course to raise money for their youth mission trips. We knew instantly that this was our transportation to the tournament!

He went on to explain that they did not charge but only asked for donations. We committed to do that and asked if he could wait until we checked in and he said that he would. While checking in, I prayed, "God, what would you have me give this church?" Then I remembered the Living a Better Story project. I had received $5 and had already made a contribution to another ministry. Edna also had received $5. So we just recycled the first ones. I knew I was to give Q (the young man's name) $50.

It was 1.3 miles to the course. When I handed him the money, he wanted to know if we would like him to pick us up afterwards. Yes! Was it ever a blessing to have your own shuttle drop you at the gate and pick you up! Every time we blessed them with $50, they were so appreciative. By Saturday they wanted to know the details about this thing called Living a Better Story. We told them, and they will be using that as part of their testimony when they carry the gospel of Jesus Christ to southern India between May 25–June 15, 2010.

God blessed us with this trip to the Masters abundantly—more than we could have ever asked or thought. It was wonderful. There were angels around us everywhere, directing our steps. The twenty-one young people from Crossroads Church were just a part of it. God is so good!

—*Kay Winslette and Edna Holland*

Ask, and it will be given to you; search, and you will find; knock, and the door will be opened for you. For everyone who asks receives, and everyone who searches finds, and for everyone who knocks, the door will be opened. Is there anyone among you who, if your child asks for bread, will give a stone? Or if the child asks for a fish, will give a snake? If you then, who are evil, know how to give good gifts to your children, how much more will your Father in heaven give good things to those who ask him!
Matthew 7:7-11

Letting Go and Letting God

I RECEIVED THE Living a Better Story envelope with a $10 bill the first week the envelopes were distributed. With faith in God and my own Type-A-personality bullheadedness, I was anxious to see what I could to with the money. Several realistic probabilities swirled around my head as I tried to settle on an idea that I could implement to make this thing work. Because of our lack of time, the envelope and its contents remained in trust for an uncharacteristically long time.

First, one week passed, and then another, as I continually tried to come up with an idea I could put into action. Finally, this past weekend my wife Kelly and I discussed what we could do. For some time, I had been wanting to make a donation to help feed the hungry. I suggested matching God's money to make a donation to the Nashville Rescue Mission (NRM). We could easily calculate the number of meals we could provide based on the publicized cost of an individual meal. This would be a quick way to grow the money in consideration of our other responsibilities. But neither Kelly nor I had the information to make this donation.

The next Sunday evening, March 7, we finally read the packet—or rather I read the packet aloud, while Kelly juggled supper for us and we considered what we could do.

I began the specific prayer discipline for this project but still continued to set about grandiose plans of what I could do, pondering connections and favors and the most elaborate schemes to work this up, all the time realizing the amount of time my family really could not spare. When I got home from work that evening, I picked up the mail from the mailbox and about passed out right there in the driveway. Right in the middle of the bills, coupons, newsletters, and cards was a solicitation envelope from Nashville Rescue Mission. I can honestly say neither Kelly nor I remember making a donation to NRM in such a way for them to get our mailing address. While the cynic might say this is coincidence and the result of commercial mailing lists, I do not think the timing was coincidence.

To further rebut the idea of coincidence, the night before I had told Kelly I would be paying the bills on Monday—the night I had set aside to have the checkbook out and the same night we ultimately received the envelope from NRM. Matching God's money, we bought meals for twenty hungry persons for a total of $46.

Although we more than quadrupled God's money, the total amount may not be earthshaking. But what was soul shaking was seeing God quickly step in and take over for me, a man obsessed with doing it all. By letting go and letting God, we experienced a truly awesome demonstration of his power. May he so guide and direct all our lives. Thanks be to God!

—*Paul and Kelly Duty*

Trust God!

I WAS AT CHURCH the day the Living a Better Story experience began, but I had to leave before the sermon to pick up a scout who was returning home from camping. When I heard about it later, I thought how neat it would be to do, but I was so far behind in everything, and this was just going to add to the already impossible task of catching up. I thought at least I had a good excuse. I'd been really ill for a couple of months from some medications I was taking. So sitting back and watching the story unfold without me was a no-brainer!

I heard about the leftover envelopes during the Wednesday Bible study and realized I still could join in if I wanted to, but I still was not feeling good. As I thought about it, I felt like I was preventing my kids from experiencing Living a Better Story if I did not do it. With my eldest currently going through confirmation, it just did not feel right. I told the kids about Living the Better Story and asked if they wanted to participate, which they did. I explained that they would be instrumental in all aspects and that it was not going to be something that I did and they watched. The next Sunday it was announced that there were still envelopes left, and we each drew an envelope.

The total amount we received was $55. After reading the lesson, talking about it, and praying for three days, we finally got together to discuss what we wanted to do with the money. There were lots of grandiose ideas at first, but I reminded them that we only had $55 and a very short time frame, and this had to be something that they could do (not me). They finally settled on the idea of getting donations for Haiti by offering free brownies, cookies, and hot chocolate or lemonade (depending on the weather) during the first weekend of soccer games on Saturday.

Normally, I am a major planner, down to every detail. I had to keep telling myself that this was God's money, everything will be fine, just let the kids figure it all out. I had to tell myself that a lot!

Then, while trying to replace some old, dusty, broken pieces of a floral arrangement and not having much luck, I finally had to take the whole thing apart and decided to go ahead and really clean the outside. I finished and then dumped out the little broken pieces that were still inside it. When I did, I noticed something stuck to the inside of the vase. I hit the side of the vase and out popped a rock onto the carpet with the words "Trust God" staring up at me! I have no idea how long that rock had been in there. I do remember the rock from church, but I cannot remember which event it came from. And how it came to land in the flower arrangement, truly, only God knows. But it was exactly what I needed to see. Trust God!

I took the kids shopping for groceries without knowing exactly how much everything would cost or how much of everything we could buy with the money we had been given. Trust God!

The kids decided how much we needed of everything on our list with very little help. After we had all our supplies, I added everything together to see if we needed to take anything back, and it had all worked out perfectly. Trust God!

Saturday soccer was rained out, but my son's tae kwon do tournament was not. Teaching moment for the kids: when one door closes, a window opens. Trust God!

What did we get out of this experience? The kids learned that even they can use the gifts and talents that God has given them to do something to help others even as far away as Haiti, all by themselves. It gave them a feeling of pride and accomplishment. Trust God!

As for me, even though I did trust God before, the visual reminder gave me the added boost I really needed to keep the faith. He truly is my rock (which I keep in my pocket or nearby). If I had taken the easy way out, I would have denied my children this stop on their spiritual journey, my ability to witness it, and other people's opportunity to witness what the kids were trying to do. And we get all of this from trying to help someone else. How great is that!

—*Debi O'Neil*

Just How God Intended

WE RECEIVED $15 AND decided to buy a Bible for a new believer. I went into a store to purchase the Bible, and I overheard a lady at the register mention a 25 percent-off card she had that was getting ready to expire, so she gave it to the cashier. It took me about an hour to decide which Bible to get, but I ended up with the Charles Stanley Life Principles Bible because it was easy to read with life applications and index tabs. The cost was $79.99, so my plan was to use $15 of God's money and pay the rest. When it was my turn to check out, the cashier used the lady's coupon on my purchase and saved me $20, which she could have used on anyone before me, so I knew that was a moment of God's favor.

The other cool part was the note we received from the recipient of the Bible. He said, "I was very surprised and a little speechless when I saw you had given me a Bible, something I never would have bought on my own. I'm not the religious type or thought I would be involved with a church again, but here I am with Biker Church of Asheville. I never would have imagined I would have been saved, but I was. I never thought I would own a Bible of any kind, but now I own one thanks to you. I'm not the kind of person who open up a Bible and read it, but you never can tell, especially how things have happened in the recent past. My friend from Biker Church says it's a really good, down-to-earth-type Bible that explains things in ways many of us can understand. It is nice to know it is here if and when I need it or could learn a little from it. Just thought I would be straight up with you about your extremely very thoughtful gift and about my life."

That was the end of his note. It made me realize that the money was spent just how God intended, because it was the Holy Spirit who drew the new believer to the Lord to be saved, and the Holy Spirit will prompt him to open up God's Word and grow in his newfound faith.

—*Theresa and Dakota Payne*

Can Openers for Hope

$\mathcal{I}$ HAD A LOT of ideas when I first received $5 of God's money. I spent time in prayer and contemplation trying to decide which area would yield the best result. Then the floods happened.

Every time I prayed, I was led right back to helping the flood victims, but I could not decide how or for what. When my family volunteered at the shelter and donation center, we saw the tremendous needs of the people. At church on Sunday, Pastor Jeremy gave a list of things that were desperately needed. One of those things struck a chord with me: can openers. We were giving out a lot of canned food, but some of these people did not have a can opener to open them.

I used God's money and some of my own to buy can openers. It felt right. A simple device that can take away a lot of worry and help a family in need. This was a wonderful, humbling, emotional journey. I'm thankful for this opportunity to Live a Better Story and strengthen my relationship with God.

—*Connie Zumbrunnen*

Running with a Purpose

I RECEIVED THE MONEY on Friday, April 16, and began praying about the most prudent manner God would have me invest it. However, while running today in Centennial Park with a friend who is not yet a believer, God prompted me to recognize the immediate need of a homeless woman.

Although I had not yet invested the Living a Better Story money ($20), the Holy Spirit directed me to give it to the homeless woman. As I gave it to her, I spoke to her and prayed God's blessing for her life. She was humbly grateful.

My friend witnessed this, and I informed him that I had an opportunity to share Jesus and his blessings with a person in need. The homeless woman, my unsaved friend, and I were all blessed by this opportunity. I am humbly grateful to be used as God's vessel in this stewardship endeavor.

—*Brent Kreid*

Sharing Out
of Experience

I WANTED TO DO this because children at Vanderbilt Children's Hospital sometimes do not have movies to watch. I know this because I go there every year when I have an asthma attack. I took God's $5 and bought a movie at Target. I asked my friends to give me movies they do not watch anymore. I am still collecting movies and will have my mom take them to the emergency room for me. Doing this project helped me feel that God loved me, and he sent me this project for a purpose. It made me feel good to help the other sick kids.

—*Daniel Head*

Cookie for a Cause

I MADE QUADRUPLE CHOCOLATE COOKIES to sell to the staff at Schmitt Elementary School in Columbus, Indiana, where I am a first grade teacher. Most people put $1 in the envelope for a bag of cookies, but a few put in $2. I invested the money in the emergency fund at our school.

Our school has around seven hundred students and has a very high rate of free and reduced-cost lunches. We have more than a 35 percent turnover rate during the school year. We have many children who are homeless, in and out of foster care, living in a facility for domestic violence victims, etc. Our emergency funds help when a child's home burns and they have no clothes, when they have fled in the middle of the night to escape an abusive situation, kids who have no school supplies, no clothes, no winter coat, no shoes, etc.

At first I was thrilled to get a chance to be part of your Living a Better Story. Then I spent a lot of time trying to decide what I could do to multiply the money and where I would invest the money. I sent an e-mail to our school staff to explain what I was doing and to ask for their help by buying cookies. I had several comments about what a wonderful idea Living a Better Story is.

I felt good about what I did, but I felt bad about not making a larger sum of money. I am giving the information about your project to the pastor at the United Methodist Church in Greenwood, Indiana, which I attend. I would like to see us be able to continue your idea and get people here involved. I have felt blessed to be a part of it and to know that others would also. It is such a wonderful way to share God's love!

—*Carol Miller*

The Sweetness of God's Word

AT FIRST I THOUGHT I wanted to donate the money to Vanderbilt Children's Hospital, but it was clear to me within a week that I was supposed to spread the Word of God with Bibles. I shared the story of our project at church the same Sunday the packets were distributed. Immediately, my parents each gave me $5, so now my money was tripled within hours. Now it was up to me to decide how to multiply it even more.

I decided that I would purchase Hershey candy bars and sell them for a donation. Who knew that people would give $5, $6, and even $10 for a plain Hershey candy bar?! It was exciting for me to see how generous others were when they learned that I would be purchasing Bibles with the money. People who did not realize how the Gideon organization works would say, "I know of some children who do not have a Bible, if you could include them that would be wonderful. They could really use a Bible." So I've made a note of those children, and I will be purchasing special Bibles just for them.

I decided to purchase the Hershey candy bars because we visited Hershey, Pennsylvania, a few years ago and learned of the Hershey Trust Company, Hershey Foundation, and Hershey School Trust. Since this goes to help disadvantaged children receive good homes and education, I thought it would be a great way to help more than one charity with the same project! Through this experience I see God working in people's lives through his Word!

—*Teresa Bishop*

A Mountain T.O.P. Experience

ONE OF OUR YOUTH members has been given the opportunity to be a Mountain T.O.P. staff member this year, and we have been trying to help her raise her half of her salary in order to go. I have seen other young lives transformed by this opportunity and cannot wait to see how her life will be changed as well! The $10 I gave inspired others in my Sunday school class to match the same amount, enabling us to raise $110 in our class alone! This experience made me realize that I have to stop and listen more often. God's voice is there, but so many times I keep asking and asking, and I'm not quiet long enough to hear the answer.

—*Pam Buck*

"This experience made me realize that I have to stop and listen more often. God's voice is there, but so many times I keep asking and asking, and I'm not quiet long enough to hear the answer."

Washing Cars, Empowering Kids

SEVERAL MEMBERS OF THE FRESHMEN Brentwood High basketball team and some of their friends had a car wash at a fast-food restaurant. They gave the money to Harvest Hands to sponsor basketball teams for their Empower Basketball League. We will be delivering the check and several basketballs this week.

Harvest Hands had been on my mind for a while, so when this opportunity presented itself, I took the time to pray about it to make sure it was what God wanted. When nothing else presented itself, I took that as God's green light to run with it and contacted the boys and their parents. I lured them to a meeting at Sonic with an offer of ice cream, but it was not necessary. They were very excited to help these kids and came up with several ideas on how to do it. The car wash idea was chosen, and the boys and some of the parents showed up on a cool Saturday morning and washed cars for six hours. They raised $853. My hope is that this experience will be a small seed for each of these boys to live a better story.

—*Kim Jones*

Ask a Question, Get an Answer

I RECEIVED $5 AND used God's money to purchase envelopes and stamps, and I am now writing letters to homebound folks from our congregation on a regular basis. This experience helped me listen to God better. I was able to ask him a direct question (What do you want me to do with your money?) and within a few days I received a very clear answer. This experience also helped me to start thinking about needs other than my own.

—*Katy Coffer*

"It was an amazing experience. We should all live our life mind-set this way on a daily basis."

—*Dana and Michael White*

It Just Felt Right

I SOLD ALL MY baby gear in the BUMC kid's sale and made $220. I had been holding on to all my baby stuff, even knowing that a third baby was not in the mix for us. I just could not get rid of it. After praying about what to do with the $20 I received of God's money, I had the idea of selling my baby things. I did not know how I would feel after unloading all of it, but walking away from all those cute baby boy clothes, the bouncy chair my boys spent hours in, the crib bedding, etc., I almost had a small panic attack. What if I made a mistake? Remembering that the money I made from selling it would help the Second Harvest Food Bank, and 30 percent of it went back to my church, well, that instantly calmed my nerves and it felt right. I know nothing drastic or life changing happened in this exchange, but it did feel good to impact several areas of ministry with just $20 and an idea.

—*Amy Cochran*

Rich in Christ

MY COUSINS GORDON AND Andrea Schnarrs, who attend Brentwood UMC, sent us two unopened envelopes and offered us the opportunity to Live a Better Story. So this is my story.

A dear friend in Pennsylvania has been truly going through some trials. She has serious health problems, she's lost her home, and her husband has been arrested for threatening her and two of her children. Because there is no money coming in, the bills have been piling up. The two Living a Better Story envelopes (one for me and one for my husband) that we received contained $5 each. My friend's car insurance was due on April 30, and we gave our $10 plus added $50 of our own to help her pay her insurance.

By walking through this experience with my friend, God has shown me that no matter what we do, he is still the one in control and that his love never fails! Thank you so much for this opportunity to share this money with others. Most of us that do not have much are still rich in Christ and are able to help fellow believers in their time of need.

—*Jody Schnarrs*

Trust in the LORD and do good; dwell in the land and enjoy safe pasture.
Psalm 37:3

Opened Eyes

MY HUSBAND AND I talked and prayed over this, wondering where God wanted me to use the $15 we received. It is so amazing to see how God opens your eyes to things around you. I started noticing how the Nashville Rescue Mission kept popping up around me—tons of television commercials, billboards, and even random people at work started talking about volunteering. I have never noticed something like this before. I knew that it was God answering our prayers and letting us know that this is where the money was to go. We knew that our own money was tight—just having had a baby only a few months ago—but we knew that matching the initial funds would feed those who were less fortunate than we.

We donated our money and feed over twenty people, and now I feel as though I am to start volunteering as well. I have been in contact with the Nashville Rescue Mission to be put on their kitchen schedule. It is so amazing how God opens your eyes, especially when you ask for his guidance.

—*Jennifer and Tim Ward*

Letters for Schools

MY ENVELOPE HAD $5 in it. I decided to write a letter to eleven of my neighbors. I explained about Living a Better Story and then told them that my heart was with the Central Asia Institute. It was established by Greg Mortenson after he began building schools for girls in Pakistan and Afghanistan. I read his book *Three Cups of Tea* last year and think that the work that is being done through the institute is the work of God's kingdom on earth. Many of my neighbors agreed with me!

There is so much going on in my personal life right now that it was daunting to think about adding anything more. It took much more than three days in prayer before I believed this is what I should and could do. I'm sure I would not have been creative or brave enough to send those letters out without God's prompting me. My neighbors are wonderful and friends, but we have a no-soliciting policy and I did not want to break the law of the neighborhood. Some laws can be broken though! I'm glad I listened to God's prompting. I always am!

—*Shirley Paris*

Fruit of the Spirit

OUR FAMILY RECEIVED THREE envelopes with $5 each. We made arrangements with Nine Fruits Smoothies for them to give $1 of every smoothie sold for a five-day period to the family of Emmett Stallings. Emmett is the husband of our daughter's physics teacher at Brentwood Academy. He is thirty years old and the father of a two-year-old. He has been recently diagnosed with stage-four liver cancer.

My daughter Kristin and her friends approached the young men who own Nine Fruits, and they agreed to help the Stallings family. Our $15 was used to print signs and purchase a donation basket. Participating in this experience really made us feel like the hands and feet of Christ. It was especially rewarding to watch my daughter and her friends respond to a tragedy with love and support for a special teacher.

—*Ellen and Steve Adams*

Whoever can be trusted with very little can also be trusted with much,
and whoever is dishonest with very little will also be dishonest with much.
So if you have not been trustworthy in handling worldly wealth,
who will trust you with true riches?
Luke 16:9-11

The Smallest Efforts

E RECEIVED $25 AND we made jewelry to sell. Our total investment was $103 in 61st Avenue UMC. I realized from this project that, as I grow in my relationship to God, I have a desire to do more, but I do not always know where to start. This experience helped me realize that even the smallest efforts can affect others. It has inspired me to ask my family to work on a quarterly family mission. (There are four of us.) Each family member will have a turn to determine what our project will be, whether it is picking up trash to help God's earth, simply writing notes, or expanding God's money to help others. I hope that it will enhance our relationship with God, each other, and the community.

—*Beverly Tudor*

Just Ask!

I SPENT A WEEK praying about what to do with God's $5. One person kept coming to my mind: a co-worker and friend who was diagnosed with breast cancer in August and had to take the year off from work. She is one of many friends who have been diagnosed recently with breast cancer.

I felt led to raise money for this cause. I sent an e-mail to all my co-workers at the school where I work and told them what our church asked us to do. I told them that I was going to give God's $5 to the Susan G. Komen Foundation in our colleague's name and asked if anyone else would like to donate. I received $135!

I felt really great about this. I was so amazed at how just asking for something could lead to something wonderful. Thank you for this opportunity to get outside of my little world and do something for someone else. It made me realize the power of prayer and that sometimes it takes some time to hear what God is telling you. It made me start to think about what I could do outside of myself.

I have always been so busy with work and my kids that it just never seemed like I had time to do anything for anyone else. This experience has made me realize that it is worth taking some time and resources and giving to someone else. Thanks for this opportunity!

—Jodi Clarke

Building a Foundation of Giving

Y TWO LITTLE BOYS and I received a total of $30 of God's money. We are going to have an outdoor family movie night on our back lawn once the weather is warm enough. We will be asking for a donation of $5 per family. We will use the $30 to prepare invitations and combine it with some of our money to provide popcorn and soft drinks for our guests.

My children—seven-year-old Will and five-year-old James—are familiar with the Harvest Hands Community Development Center, because we regularly support their after-school program by providing snacks each month. They felt strongly about giving our contribution to Harvest Hands. When we looked on the Harvest Hands Web site, we were excited to see that they are trying to raise $5,000 by June. We look forward to being a part of that. We are very excited about feeling empowered and challenged to make a difference.

This project has provided a wonderful opportunity for us as a family to talk about being the hands and feet of God in a very real way. I'm thankful to have my children involved in something they can understand at such a young age. It's a great opportunity for them to build on for the rest of their lives.

—*Amy Fox*

Basketballs for Hope

I STARTED A CAMPAIGN at my office to raise money for the Jimmy V Foundation for Cancer Research. I joined the Show Your Spirit Campaign that the foundation had established for March Madness. In this campaign, I sold basketballs for $5 in memory of or in honor of survivors to be displayed on a wall in our front office. Everyone was encouraged to wear their team shirt on March 24 for $5 and to wear jeans for $1 each Friday for the rest of the year. From thirty-six employees, we raised $1,250, and my company agreed to match the amount. On March 24, I am using my $5 toward fixing sandwiches for everyone who participated and celebrating our participation in this campaign.

Cancer is a disease that touches almost every person. It was miraculous to see how everyone rallied to raise money for this cause. It was important to everyone that all of the money was directed to research. It was a blessing to see how many truly made a sacrificial donation because they had been so deeply affected by the loss of a loved one or friend. The most moving testimony was a co-worker who had us enlarge the size of the basketball we were using, because his sixteen-year-old daughter was a survivor of leukemia for five years. He is a strong Christian and gave a wonderful testimony to God's blessings.

It also humbled me to see on more than one occasion that those who could afford the least gave the most. It certainly reminded me what joy and fulfillment you can feel from working for a purpose that benefits others. And without a doubt that is what God would have us do.

—*Trina Thomas*

O Lord my God,

Teach my heart this day where and how to see you,

Where and how to find you.

You have made me and remade me,

And you have bestowed on me

All the good things I possess,

And still I do not know you.

I have not yet done that

For which I was made.

Teach me to seek you,

For I cannot seek you

Unless you teach me,

Or find you

Unless you show yourself to me.

Let me seek you in my desire,

Let me desire you in my seeking.

Let me find you by loving you,

Let me love you when I find you.

—ST. ANSELM

The Least of These

MY DAUGHTER AND I purchased two cases of water and a bag of trash bags. We invited New Covenant and parents of teens' Sunday school classes to serve with us by bagging mulch and woodchips for homeless people to use as kindling in their tent city. We also shared cases of water with them. Thirteen people came, representing seven families.

After bagging the mulch, we put the bags on a trailer and loaded all the extra wood in another truck. The homeless use the wood chips and extra wood to keep warm and to cook their food. After we unloaded the mulch and wood chips for kindling, we divided into groups. The adults used a chainsaw to cut some larger pieces of wood for better burning, while some other adults and the teens cleaned a trash dump area and mulched a walkway to a tent in a very muddy area. The residents were friendly and helpful. It was great that they would share their needs with us.

A father and son went back on Sunday with sleeping bags, clothes, and more. We also brought leftover desserts from an event at the church. The homeless loved it!

With Matthew 25 as my inspiration, while we were serving, I made a concerted effort to see each person in the tent city as if he or she were Jesus. I had never tried this before. I wanted to look on them, not with pity or fear, but rather to see the love I have for Jesus shining on them. Each need we see and each person we meet is put there so we can serve Jesus.

—*Kelly Gilfillan*

Money for Sick Days

MY FIRST REACTION TO this experiment was apprehension. What could I do? I knew in my heart that the actual giving away of the money would not be a problem, but how could the money be multiplied? Like a lot of people, we're caught in the crunch of caretaking children and parents plus working, so the idea of taking on a money-making project, honestly, just was overwhelming. However, we knew God...

After the three days, I experienced a great desire to multiply the money. The answer came in an e-mail at work when an opportunity arose to sell back some sick-day hours! Wow! I knew this was the way—a personal sacrifice was what we were called to make. So that is how $10 turned into $300.

What should I do with the money? We were led to give it in three ways: personally, locally, and nationally. So the original $10 was used to encourage a struggling caretaker by getting her out to lunch. The rest of the money was equally divided among the Nashville Rescue Mission, the Great Smoky Mountains (celebrating God's creation), and a grocery gift card for a family that is struggling with job losses.

We hope that our hearts will be opened to others and how we as individuals can help with something as simple as a smile or recognize when someone needs your time to listen. We were reminded of how often we take for granted all the blessings that God gives us every day.

—*Patricia Ladnier*

It's Not About the Money

OUR FAMILY (NORMAN, ANNA, Abigail, and Will) started by praying for three days and thinking that we had to find a way to multiply the dollars to do some good for someone else. In the beginning we focused only on the money, even though we heard Reverend Cliff say, "It's not about the money."

It was after the second week that we began to think we were either not praying about it correctly or we were not allowing ourselves to listen to God. Recently we had visited Bethany Health Care Center, and as a family we kept thinking that we should do something meaningful for the persons we encountered there.

After almost two weeks of praying, our sophomore daughter suggested that perhaps we needed to consider a service project that had meaning to the residents at Bethany instead of trying to turn our $5 into some amount of money. So we hand-made get-well cards, putting verses and drawing pictures inside that we hoped would bring light to some of the residents. We purchased small hand creams, combs, tissues, etc., placed the items inside Ziploc bags, and delivered them along with some kind words and conversation.

The time our second-grade son and tenth-grade daughter spent with the residents meant more to them than any amount of money we could ever have given to this wonderful facility that provides a permanent home to some and temporary rehabilitation for others.

—*The Sparks Family*

More Time for Family

HAVE PRAYED OVER the money but still not heard God speaking to me regarding how it should be used. I have given my time and money to several organizations in the past few weeks and have listened intently, but I do not feel like God was calling me to give them his $5. I will continue to be patient and pray until God lets me know how he wants it to be used.

Money aside, the Living a Better Story experience has changed my life and the lives of my family members. We are in the process of making some significant life changes to focus less on our things and more on our time with one another and a renewed focus on God.

I am considering a new job, which includes a significant pay decrease, in order to spend more time with my family and do something that I enjoy. I do not want my story to be that I journeyed to wherever my salary would increase. I want to worship God, not my money. This thought brings me to tears, because I know there have been times when the money came first. I cannot tell you how excited my family is as we enter this time in our lives.

—*Anonymous*

Growing Goodness

I USED THE $5 I received to buy vegetable seeds to help an eighty-two-year-old man plant and tend a garden. This elderly gentleman has had a garden all his life and is no longer able to plant and take care of it. He loves to watch it grow and eat the fresh vegetables. His wife is an excellent cook, and I get to eat fresh vegetables with them quite often. Every year he tells me we are not going to plant next year, but when the time comes to break the ground, he asks, "When are we going to break the garden?"

The good Lord has blessed me with good health and stamina, so I get at it! I also get a lot of pleasure in watching the garden grow and giving fresh food to others! It makes me walk closer with God every day and gives me exercise to stay healthy so that I can do it again next year!! This year, I plan on giving Graceworks some of our harvest.

—*David Fowler*

Amazingly God!

THIS HAS BEEN THE most amazing experience because the more stories I hear and the more I tell my own, the more I've felt God's presence surrounding me and those who were blessed enough to hear about the experience. When the Living a Better Story experience started, I totally missed the introduction at church. I thought the packets were instructions to put together a shoebox of goodies to send to the needy.

I brought my packet home and later thought how busy I was and started to throw it away. I was at work when I opened it, and Wow! It had $20 in it! I thought, What a great thing, they even gave me money to buy the goodies to go in the shoebox. Then I started reading. I immediately got scared, because anyone who knows me knows that I am financially needy. I am so empty-handed. I thought to myself, If I could have multiplied money, don't you think I would have done that already?

I fought off the nagging temptation to come up with something on my own. I disciplined myself to ask God for help every time the fear of failure and pride crept in. For almost a week, I prayed and waited. Then I remembered a little box of gold jewelry I had. I had only a few pieces and would never go to any of the gold parties that my friends were having, because I really did not have enough to bother with. I took it to the mall to try to sell and prayed that God would double it. God took what was broken and worthless and handed me back $240. That's so amazingly God!

—*Melinda Nathan*

Faith and Roller Coasters

THIS HAS BEEN THE most powerful spiritual experience my family has shared together. It is deeply personal and has created a true desire in us to Live a Better Story. Listening to God speak has brought us closer to friends who are facing similar spiritual challenges. God has thus far made it clear that we do not have to act alone but can count on others (and they can count on us) to seek his will. It's like standing in line with a group of friends to ride the scariest roller coaster for the first time. I'd easily jump out of line and never experience the thrill without their support and encouragement. It's enough excitement to make you want to run out and tackle the first need you run across.

Fortunately, we are all listening even harder to where and how God wants us to serve. We've realized the last thing we need right now is to all be in line for the ride only to get to the front to find out some of us were looking for the roller coaster while others were expecting to board Dumbo.

—*Bryan Tharpe and Family*

Face in the Window

LATE ON A RAINY night at the McDonald's drive-through downtown, a face suddenly appeared at my car window from behind the menu board. Startled, instinctively I quickly rolled up the window. Then when I realized it was the face of a homeless man covered in garbage bags to keep dry. I ordered food for him and tried to find him. I drove block by block in the dark and rain to find him to no avail. I was seeing the face of Jesus, hungry and alone—and I rolled up the window!

Looking now for any homeless person with which to share the food, no one was on the street due to the pouring rain, and I never was able to find the man whose face is emblazoned on my memory. I felt that Jesus personified appeared at my car window, and I failed to recognize him. This experience has raised my sensitivity to the distress of homeless people and has turned my heart toward making a difference, however small that might be.

As a result, I used my $5 to produce flyers describing the plight of homeless teens and children, and we were able to donate fifty pairs of jeans to the Rescue Mission and to allow my seven-year-old grandson to experience how a simple item such as jeans can make a difference for kids like him who need so much. Living a Better Story has been a path to reconcile that rainy night and to open my heart to God's will.

—*Debbie Jackson*

Dispensing God's Care

I RECEIVED $20 AND decided to multiply it by not eating lunch out for two weeks and adding those funds to my gift. In addition, I asked others to skip lunch for one day and donate their lunch money to the cause. The money is being donated to Dispensary of Hope (DH). DH is a non-profit that provides medication to uninsured and underinsured individuals and families. Their program provides $10 worth of medication for every $1 donated.

During my three days of prayer, I was drawn to pay attention to the issue of healthcare partly because of the amount of coverage given the topic every day on the news. As I prayed and tried to discern God's will for his gift, I sensed a need to focus specifically on medicine. I discussed a variety of ideas with different pharmacists, and one pointed me toward Dispensary of Hope. I had never heard of DH until this experience, and I am convinced that I will continue to support their mission in the future. I've contacted the director of development, and we are discussing some ideas for future fund-raising.

I feel humbled at the realization that what seems like a little is not a little when God is involved. I felt more disciplined when lunchtime rolled around. It provided me an opportunity to share with my co-workers how God was at work. The evolution of the plan was clearly the work of God, as I had never heard of DH or taken a personal interest in the medication needs of others.

—*Mike Walsh*

Editing a Better Story

*L*IKE SO MANY OTHERS, we found this exercise much more difficult to do than we initially thought. We were both hung up on multiplying the money and using our talents to do so. We read and prayed the prayer for about ten days. I was sitting at the dining room table, proofing one of the seven United Methodist calendars for 2011, when I realized that this was my talent: writing and editing. After all, I've spent many years doing that (I am the retired editor of *Pockets* for The Upper Room). I thought, we can take the money from the next calendar to come in and use it to live our story. Jim agreed to that, so that is what we did. We included the original $10 in the amount.

We felt led to invest God's money in Harvest Hands, specifically to pay the fees for children to participate in activities and field trips, since that is where our church is working to revitalize a neighborhood (and ourselves in the process). We are also participating in the efforts of two other families to grow their money and live their story. Please keep challenging us. All of us could do so much more.

—*Jim and Jan Knight*

Coming Out of My Shell

I HAVE BEEN COMING to the church for the last six months and did not have many relationships. I have found some peace, and little by little, I have found a place of support—both social and spiritual. I have been away from God for many years, but this church has been welcoming and open to my suggestions. I was hesitant to take a Living a Better Story envelope but eager to express a plan that I already had and did not know how to implement. I shared it with JoAnn Eckhardt. (I sit next to her in worship, and she helps me when I am lost in the readings or the songs at the service. She is wonderful.) We pooled our money, and I bought a magazine on how to develop Web sites easily.

As a result, we have partnered with other church members to provide some review information on the Web for Spanish students, and I will teach a specialized medical Spanish course in the fall. The services will be provided free to the church. However, I would like 50 percent of the proceeds to go to victims of natural disasters. This course will not only multiply the money with a lasting effect, but it will also teach professionals much valuable and needed information in the medical field serving a community that is sometimes underserved. I think this is a great opportunity to come out of my shell and use the great talents God has given me!

—*Alicia Rodriguez*

A Different Way of Looking at Money

I PURCHASED A PREPAID Visa card for a co-worker. She moved into her first home in early December only to find that the furnace did not work. They have kept warm with a fireplace and space heaters. She did not have money for a home inspection prior to purchase. Despite having an income level that requires her to receive food stamps, she lives with her son (who has a minimum-wage job), her daughter-in-law, her granddaughter, and two of her son's friends who have lost jobs and need a place to stay. She is a tireless worker on the job, and her co-workers are aware of her increased needs at this time. She never advertises her need or complains about her circumstances. I wanted to be able to honor her by helping her out financially. For the first three days of prayer, I looked at the money differently. I saw it as God's money. It was not my money to do something with, even for a good cause; it was God's money. I needed to look at all of my financial gifts in the same way. I was touched by the generosity of my co-workers when they heard about the fishes and loaves project I was working on. It brought one of my co-workers to tears.

—*Tim and Paula Gaddis*

The Still, Small Voice

NOTHING CAME TO ME after I prayed for direction on how to use God's money. I thought it was because I was not listening enough for God's word. But the thought kept running through my mind that he wanted me to use my skills. I do not feel creative, but all I had was this thought to use my skills. So after praying again and asking for guidance, I realized the thought was still there. I am a financial and administrative consultant to nonprofit associations, and I promised God to give two hours of my contract fee to help someone in need.

"My experience is that God's voice is very small, and you have to listen very intently and trust that what you feel, think, or hear is his true voice. This was a soul-searching exercise for me, and I think it is something I should do more often."

My experience is that God's voice is very small, and you have to listen intently and trust that what you feel, think, or hear is his true voice. This was a soul-searching exercise for me, and I think it is something I should do more often.

—*Nelle Greulich*

No Coincidences

A FTER SEVERAL DAYS OF debate, I could not figure out what to do with God's $5. Many things crossed through my mind, but nothing really stuck out. Well, this evening when I came home and checked my mail, I found a request from the Nashville Rescue Mission. To my recollection, I do not think I've ever donated to this organization, but I recall getting similar donation requests in the mail periodically. As usual, I put it and the rest of the mail on my desk at home next to my computer and planned to attend to it later.

After I turned on my computer, I searched through the church's Web site for something and noticed the Channel 5 news story that was done regarding the Living a Better Story campaign. I hit the play button, and immediately prior to the story was a video request from the Nashville mayor asking for donations to help the Nashville Rescue Mission! Within inches on my desk sat the $5 I received from BUMC, the Rescue Mission solicitation, and the video of the mayor's request for donations to the mission.

I instantly realized that God was speaking to me. So I pulled out my checkbook and gave a donation to feed twenty-five people at the rescue mission. I inserted my check in the envelope, along with the original $5 too.

A few minutes later I thought, Let me look at that Channel 5 story again and see if the Nashville Rescue Mission statement precedes the story again. Nope. I've refreshed the page four or five times. Not only was the Nashville rescue story from the mayor not there anymore, but those first fifteen seconds were all company paid advertisements. The mayor's plea was there earlier though, and that was no coincidence. That was God working in a simple, powerful way. Thankfully, I was listening.

—*Andy Voyles*

A Dollar a Day Will Pave the Way

I HAD A HARD time deciding what to do with the $10 I received and deciding how to increase God's money. I took it with me this past weekend to my parent's church in Jackson, Tennessee, to pray about it. I prayed again for guidance during the service.

After church I was looking at a display in the narthex about Lakeshore Methodist Assembly Campground—the Memphis Conference camp. I remembered all the great camps and retreats I had attended there while growing up in West Tennessee. I picked up a pamphlet that described the group's capital campaign to raise funds for new children's camps and badly needed renovations. The pamphlet was titled "A Dollar a Day Will Pave the Way." The $10 I received from BUMC got me ten days down the road to paying back Lakeshore for putting me and so many other young people on a path of discipleship for my entire life. I will match that gift with one to Beersheba Springs for all the good work they do for the Tennessee Conference. I can see that I spent too much time thinking and worrying instead of listening. When I dropped the net, a fish swam right in it! I need a little more "let go and let God" in my life.

—*Greg McClarin*

Empowering Children to Be All They Can Be!

THIS ASSIGNMENT HAS PROVIDED intentional thinking and focus on the fact that all ministry indeed starts with God. It's a wonderful reminder that in spite of our organizational skills, our planning, and our experience, all of which are good tools, everything will be brought together by the God who simply teaches us to love one another. I am pretty sure God will take this experience away from me, as he always does! I am grateful for the lessons learned. I am grateful for the challenge. This experience has widened my trust, widened how I allow God to lead, widened how I accept the end result, and widened my hope that what is provided for this planned ministry will be adequate for the need.

I received $10 in my packet and planned an open house on March 20 to sell donated goods. Any unsold items would be donated to World Relief. I hope to purchase ten digital cameras to facilitate a camera/art ministry with the children at Harvest Hands. This will include free form expressions—a way of framing their lives and their stories. My short-term goal is self-expression; my mid-term goal is affirming the children's value, shining God's light on their individual lives. Another mid-term goal is to help children develop computer skills for photo downloading and printing and networking to facilitate a gallery show at local schools, art venues, and Harvest Hands house. Exciting long-term goals include a microbusiness opportunity in making and printing note cards, bookmarks, etc. for sale and/or professional digital printing of photographs for resale. I hope to provide an atmosphere that will foster critical thinking and little instruction. I want to empower children to be all they can be!

—*Jackie Shields*

Bookmarks and Barbecue

WE PURCHASED SCRAP LEATHER with the original $5 and made bookmarks to sell to family and friends. We are still making, mailing, and collecting the donations. We also sold barbeque dinners to the Center for Children and Families so they could have a night without having to cook a meal. The first ministry is for us to purchase stuffed animals to donate to the "Olds Mobile" and the second is Amos House: a charity that helps homeless mothers and pregnant women on the streets of Nashville.

We followed the Bible study and prayed for an answer. Trying to grasp the fact that there are seventeen hundred homeless children in Nashville, we knew we wanted to do something. After two and a half weeks, I woke up in the middle of the night thinking about Amos House and what I would do if I found myself homeless with two small children. It is a charity I heard about a week before this lesson, and it has been on my mind every day.

The Olds Mobile is a wonderful project, and we believe this is an easy and heartfelt way for our kids to show God's love and have a better understanding of his grace. (Our children are four years old and two years old).

—*Sean and Jill Stroud*

Jar of Change for Change

I WAS EXCITED TO receive my Living a Better Story envelope. My competitive nature kicked in, and I began to wonder how I could get others who were involved in the process to multiply their holdings of God's money. As is often the case, God had other plans. While I was following a daily custom and emptying a pocketful of change into a jar one evening, it struck me that I had a large jar of loose change at my fingertips. While this change had little meaning to me, it had the potential to mean a great deal to someone in need. I was convicted at that moment that this jar of change was part of God's plan. I also became certain that God was not using this exercise so that I could change others but so he could change me. Giving up the loose change was not in itself a sacrificial act, so I concluded that I should make a matching contribution equal to the amount of change in the jar.

Although I now felt clear about where God was leading me, I was uncertain about how to put God's money to work—until I read "The Beam" this morning. As I sat in the pew, I felt a great certainty about how the money would be put to use. After church, I was excited to take the jar of change to a local grocery store that has a machine to count and sort loose change. The result? After a small service charge, the net amount of the change was $154.39. With our matching funds, we had a total of almost $309. God had clearly provided an answer. A child in South Africa can attend preschool for $310!

—*Mike Mauldin*

Showing Is Better than Telling

I COMBINED MY MONEY with my mother's and daughter's money to make $25, and we purchased groceries to feed a free red-beans-and-rice lunch to my office after our sales meeting this past Wednesday. We asked for donations and received $150. I set up a PayPal account and e-mailed my office to let them have an opportunity to donate if they missed the lunch. So we may receive even more.

"This was one of the most powerful experiences I've had in church. I believe that showing is better than telling, and this experience was truly a hands-on education for me about God's power to guide, love, and bless his people."

We made a $25 contribution to the new Daily Bread Food Bank in Eagleville, Tennessee. The balance of the funds ($125+) will be donated to Harvest Hands CDC for investment in their MIMIC projects, WOW Soap, and Humphreys Street Coffee Company so God's money can continue to grow!

This was one of the most powerful experiences I've had in church. I believe that showing is better than telling, and this experience was truly a hands-on education for me about God's power to guide, love, and bless his people.

—*Dawne Davis*

Search Where Our Hearts Are Leading Us

THE MORNING AFTER CLIFF presented us with this challenge, the ladies of Brentwood were buzzing with excitement, ideas, thoughts, e-mails, prayers, and meetings. An e-mail forwarded from Caren Teichman featured a Channel 4 news story link about Amos House and how this organization tries to help the seventeen hundred homeless children in our city must have been read by close to one hundred women who kept forwarding it to their various Bible studies. This was the first tug. Later, in a parking lot, I encountered a staff member of Safe Haven who I used to be in close contact with, and we discussed how we drift away occasionally from what we have a heart for. The big tug came when I learned from her that a baby will be home at the Safe Haven Family shelter in May, another one to add to the seventeen hundred in need.

After a lunch meeting with just four women, we had an event planned that would be held at Debbie Hill's home on March 12. There will be food and fellowship for lots of ladies who need to eat lunch and can for a nominal charge for this worthy cause. This money will be spent on formula, diapers, or whatever else is on the needs and supply list that Safe Haven or Amos House can send to us via e-mail from time to time. Gimmick or not, this concept allows us to search where our hearts are leading us.

—*Jane Alger*

Help for Those
Who Help Us

M Y HUSBAND AND I moved here from northern Virginia last summer and have been regularly attending BUMC since last November. Shortly after we were each given $5 in the Living a Better Story packets, we returned to Virginia on a business trip.

While there, we went to Walter Reed Army Medical Center in DC to pick up copies of x-rays I had neglected to get before I moved. My habit while living there had been to take books to the Red Cross in the hospital for sharing with patients and family, and since we were heading to the hospital, I again delivered books.

While on the elevator, we were joined by a very young couple. I noticed that the young man had been wounded. Just observing this couple touched both of us. We thought that they had just started their life together and now faced not only the challenges of building a home and a family but also the challenges of the military way of life that included separations as well as the physical and mental challenges of going to war. How does an eighteen- or nineteen-year-old wife learn to grow with those types of challenges?

As a retired naval officer, I was familiar with working with young men and women who enlist in the service, but you can forget how very young they are. They marry, start families, and become adults at an age when so many other children are going off to college, joining fraternities, partying, and living off of mom and dad.

Our $10 was donated to the Navy and Marine Corps Relief Society. We chose Navy Relief because I have firsthand knowledge of their support for young families when they get in over their heads financially or have to deal with emergencies (which always happen while a military spouse is deployed). We contributed our own funds along with the $10. But I do not consider that we made the money grow. However, Navy Relief, through their policies of loans and grants to help families in times of need, will be able to use the money again and again, because every loan is paid back.

—Cynthia Sweet and Joseph Grosson

God,

I really want to live a better story.

You've blessed me with so many resources — health, food, shelter, gifts and talents. Yet sometimes I feel like I'm just going through the motions — sleepwalking through life, stuck in my own rut, not noticing the people around me who need your healing touch. God, please wake me up. Help me to notice other's needs and care enough to do what I can to help. Warm my heart, open my eyes, strengthen my hands. Empower me to make my life a story worth telling.

Amen.

— ANONYMOUS

A New Mattress, An Answered Prayer

OUR DAUGHTER AND A friend told us about a lady from Liberia who lives here and is in their Sunday school class. She brought her family to this country after her husband was killed in Liberia. She is a hard-working woman, but she has little money. Her mattress (which someone gave her) was absolutely worn out, and she had tried to stuff rags in it so she would have something to sleep on. My daughter told us about this last fall, and we all said that we should get this woman a mattress, but time went by and we did nothing.

Fast-forward six months: On Sunday, two weeks ago, we took an envelope and found a $5 bill in it. My first thought was about this woman's mattress. I did not have any ideas for growing the money, so we decided to take some from our savings. Sometime during the following week my daughter mentioned the mattress again. Not only did I feel the gentle nudge from God when we opened our envelope, but I feel he also spoke to us through our daughter. We decided we would join our daughter and a friend and buy this woman a new box spring and mattress.

Last Friday our daughter took the woman so she could pick out a mattress set that felt good to her. It will be delivered to her little home on Tuesday. She said she had been praying for another mattress for five years. Sometimes it takes a while for God to answer prayer, but when he does, everyone involved receives a special blessing. Needless to say, this lovely lady is thrilled with her new bed.

—*Robert and Patricia Long*

Three People, Three Needs, Three Stories

THIS PROCESS HAS MADE me more conscientious of how giving a little makes a bigger difference.

Not long after receiving God's money and praying for guidance, I had a call from a friend back home. His mother's house had flooded the same weekend that Nashville had flooded. I thought for a couple of seconds about how much we could afford to send, but I was overwhelmed with the need to send her a gift card. We could put off whatever that money would have bought us. My daughter and I immediately picked up a gift card to send her. I added some money to the $10. Her son told us later that receiving this gift gave his mother hope that things were going to be okay.

At the end of May, my daughter and I moved across town. On one of our many moving days I stopped at a Waffle House for dinner. I always order too much food there. My bill came to around $10. I had a ten and a twenty in my wallet. I laid down the ten as the tip and got up to check out. The waitress took the money and my check from the table. I stopped her and said that the money was for her and handed her the twenty to pay the bill. She replied that the money was very needed and thanked me.

I can feel it coming on faster to do these kinds of things. I'm not wrestling with "should I or not." A lady's car bumped into mine at McDonald's one morning. We got out and agreed that everything was okay. She apologized and said she was having a terrible morning. I paid for her breakfast as I went through the line in front of her. I trust that her day was better because of this, maybe just a little. But I had to do it. I could not drive off without doing it.

Those are three of the changes in my life. Hopefully these individual stories are better because I listened to the small, still voice.

—*Julie Lewis*

All the $20 Bills

WHEN I OPENED MY envelope from God and found $20, I was so excited to prove to God how much I could do with his money. Then I stressed for quite some time about how to grow the money to make more of an impact. I thought if I could find a cause, a way to grow the money might follow. The only thing growing, however, was my stress. I listened for God to tell me how to do this to be most pleasing to him, but all I heard was, "In my time, not yours." I felt pressured to complete my project within the allotted time. So many people had wonderful ideas and grew their money in leaps and bounds. I was envious that I was not as productive.

I teach in an inner-city high school where new needs are revealed each day. One day after school, a young girl of fourteen—Stephany—missed her bus and did not have a way to get home. She was nearly in tears and told me that she was a new student and did not even know if she could tell me where she lived. I calmed her and told her that I would take her home, that somehow we'd find the way.

Stephany and I drove around town for quite some time trying to find out which motel she called home. During that time she revealed more of her story to me. She and her brother and sister had recently been removed from her mother's home by the Department of Children's Services. They were now living with her father, who had recently taken a job selling meat on a route that sometimes took him to Kentucky and sometimes to Alabama. He was on the road most of the time, and the kids stayed home by themselves after school. If her father had a good day on the route, he would have money to bring home something to eat. An even better week was when he could pay the motel by the week instead of by the night.

Since the majority of the students in this high school receive free lunches, I asked Stephany if she was receiving the lunches. She told me that she had not because her dad had not had the time to complete the forms. This child had not eaten all day! When I finally found the motel, I was appalled at the surroundings: they lived on the ground floor, and her father had left the sliding glass door unlocked all day so that the kids could come in after school. There was a crowd of men standing outside the motel and drinking from brown paper bags. Stephany told me that she had to walk past those men twice a day to catch the bus. Leaving Stephany at that hotel was the hardest thing I'd ever done.

"I finally learned the lesson God wanted me to learn: he provides every $20 bill that I have."

I called the police department to report the loitering. I called the school transportation office to report a dangerous bus stop. And I called the school lunch program to implement the free lunch program for this family—but it would take approximately a week to begin. I could not sleep all night for thinking about this family. Then God finally gave me the answer I'd been seeking. He asked me what I'd done with the $20 he had given me? Of course, I was not growing it, but I went to the cafeteria the next morning and gave the manager $20 to cover Stephany's breakfasts and lunches until her paperwork was approved. When I told the cafeteria manager about this family, she began collecting food for me to take to them at the motel. Other teachers heard about the family and took up a collection of clothing for the children.

I felt good about the way I used God's money, but he was not finished with me yet. One day in church, they took up a special collection for Habitat for Humanity. God immediately asked me what I'd done with the $20 he had given me? I dropped $20 in the plate. Several times since then, I've felt God's nudging, asking me what I have done with the $20 he gave me.

I finally learned the lesson God wanted me to learn: he provides every $20 bill that I have. While I'm certainly not wealthy, God has taught me that I can afford $20 for people in need, especially since that money is only mine through God's grace.

—Sue Johnson

Better Decisions

It took me quite a while to feel God's leadership on how to invest the $10 I received for "Living a Better Story." I struggled at first, just wanting to help others and piggy-back on their ideas. Then I felt overwhelmed with the needs and possibilities that flitted through my mind. Finally, I decided to donate the money I received to Better Decisions through our church's program of Alternative Giving. I do not have a multiplied sum of money to report, but I believe the effect can be "priceless," to quote a popular commercial.

I have been a volunteer mentor with this program for women in prison for several terms and have witnessed the hope it brings to troubled lives. The ladies in prison who complete this course of study share that, for the first time in their lives, they understand how their choices led them on a cataclysmal path to incarceration. More significant is their realization that can be empowered to break out of these destructive cycles by making "better decisions" once they are released from prison. I pray that even $10, perhaps providing a student notebook, will not only help a woman change the course of her life, but the lives of her children and extended family as well.

"… I was in prison and you came to visit me." Matthew 25:36

—*Sandy Olds*

A Company Community Fund

I own a healthcare reimbursement specialty company in Franklin, Tennessee. We are a 10-year-old company with 270 employees and do business in 32 states. I spoke to my senior management team of 10 and asked them to prayerfully consider, at a minimum, matching the $10 that I received from BUMC. We also discussed what we would do with the money that we would collect. It was decided that whatever amount was collected/multiplied, it would serve as the foundation for establishing a Company Community Fund. This fund will be established to support missions and other Christian organizations in Middle Tennessee. It will also be used to assist our employees with financial support on a need basis. These needs will be heard by a committee of the company and funds will be used to help our employees that struggle with issues that have been brought upon them through unfortunate circumstances. This Community Fund will stay in perpetuity and as our company continues to grow and have success, we will contribute profits into this fund. Our goal is to have a Community Fund well into the 6 digits by the end of this year!

This has been a great experience. Thank you for allowing me to participate.

—*Stuart McWhorter*

CONTRIBUTORS

Abramson, Lisa
Adams, Ellen & Steve
Alger, Jane
Anderson, Linda & Norm
Ballesteros, Cheryl
Bartels, Mary Lou & Marvin
Bishop, Teresa
Buck, Pam
Chance, Trina & Bob
Clarke, Jodi
Cochran, Amy
Cochran, Katherine & Don
Coffer, Katy
Davis, Dawne
DeMumbrum, Carol
Dennison, Mike
Duty, Kelly & Paul
Eddlemon, Brenda & Tom
Erickson, Jane & John
Fisher, Holly
Fowler, David
Fox, Amy
Gaddis, Paula & Tim

Gilfillan, Kelly
Glaus, Dianne
Greulich, Nelle
Gwinn, Rachel
Hall, Lucinda
Hassall, Kelly & Hal
Head, Daniel
Holland, Edna
Hollis Family
Hollis, Karrie
Hoover, Patricia
Horner, Cheryl & Roger
Hubbard, S.
Jackson, Debbie
Jackson, Shirley & Gary
James, Melissa
Johnson, Sue
Jones, David,
Jones, Kim
Kiser, LeAnn Olliff
Knestrick, Gracie
Knight, Jan & Jim
Knudsen, Richard G.

CONTRIBUTORS

Kolaks, Elaine & Sonny
Kreid, Brent
Ladnier, Patricia
Lamb, James R.
Latto Family
Lewis, Julie
Long, Patricia & Robert
Massengale, Mary
Mauldin, Mike
McGaughey, Mary
McLarin, Greg
McWhorter, Stuart
Melton, Rachael
Miller, Carol
Murrell, Holly & Hal
Nathan, Melinda
Nussmeyer, Ann & Mark
Olds, Sandy
O'Neil, Debi
Paris, Shirley
Patterson, Pam & Ron
Payne, Gina & Phillip
Payne, Theresa & Dakota
Peak, Marlane

Peden, Michele
Rodriguez, Alicia
Roth, Nashon
Rothhaar, Laura & Tom
Sager, Kris
Schnarrs, Andrea & Gordon
Schnarrs, Jody
Shields, Jackie
Sparks Family
Stroud, Sean & Jill
Sullins, Robert M.
Sweet, Cynthia & Grosson, Joseph
Tharpe, Brian & Family
Thomas, Trina
Troutman, Linda
Tucker, Brian
Tudor, Beverly
Voyles, Andy
Wade, Kimberly & John
Walsh, Mike
Ward, Jennifer & Tim
Watson, Ben
Winslette, Kaye & Holland, Edna
Zumbrunnen, Connie

See for Yourself How
You Can Live a Better Story

If reading these stories has inspired you to live a better story yourself, please check out the "Living a Better Story" page on our website: www.bumc.net/LABS. You'll find a link to print your own "Living a Better Story" packet and directions for participating in this potentially life-changing experience. Go ahead—see for yourself what God can do when we focus our attention on the needs of others. We would welcome the chance to hear about your experience as well. Send us your story at www.bumc.net/LABS and click on the link, "Share Your Story."

Brentwood United Methodist Church

309 Franklin Road
Brentwood, Tennessee 37027
615.373.3663
www.bumc.net

LaVergne, TN USA
28 October 2010

202538LV00004B/6/P